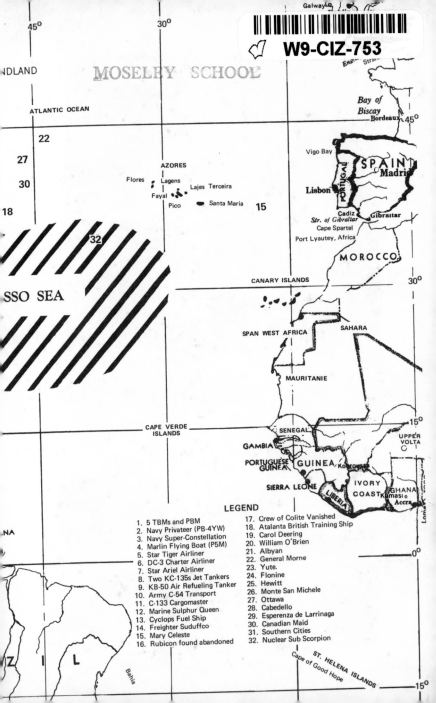

MOSELEY SCHOOL

LEGEND

1. 5 TBMs and PBM
2. Navy Privateer (PB-4YW)
3. Navy Super-Constellation
4. Marlin Flying Boat (P5M)
5. Star Tiger Airliner
6. DC-3 Charter Airliner
7. Star Ariel Airliner
8. Two KC-135s Jet Tankers
9. KB-50 Air Refueling Tanker
10. Army C-54 Transport
11. C-133 Cargomaster
12. Marine Sulphur Queen
13. Cyclops Fuel Ship
14. Freighter Suduffco
15. Mary Celeste
16. Rubicon found abandoned

17. Crew of Colite Vanished
18. Atalanta British Training Ship
19. Carol Deering
20. William O'Brien
21. Albyan
22. General Morne
23. Yute.
24. Flonine
25. Hewitt
26. Monte San Michele
27. Ottawa
28. Cabedello
29. Esperanza de Larrinaga
30. Canadian Maid
31. Southern Cities
32. Nuclear Sub Scorpion

LIMBO OF THE LOST

LIMBO
OF THE
LOST

Written by:

JOHN WALLACE SPENCER

Actual Stories of Sea Mysteries

PHILLIPS PUBLISHING COMPANY
WESTFIELD, MASS. 01085

Second printing .... October, 1969

Published in 1969 by Phillips Publishing Company
90 Elm Street, Westfield, Massachusetts 01085

Copyright 1969 by John Wallace Spencer

Manufactured in the United States of America

ABOUT THE AUTHOR

John Wallace Spencer is a man of diversified interests who makes those around him understand that he will not tolerate the "fighting of knowledge." Along the way to his present position as General Manager of WDEW, a radio station in Westfield, Massachusetts, he served for ten years in the U. S. Air Force. Worked as a postal inspector, newspaper editor, public relations director, television and radio announcer and salesman.

Research, history, writing and UFO investigation are hobbies of long standing. He has lived and worked in Massachusetts, New York, Mississippi, Tennessee, New Jersey, Iowa, Connecticut, England and Germany.

Mr. Spencer became interested in the "Limbo of the Lost" area when the nuclear submarine "Scorpion" disappeared in the Atlantic. Through research a pattern began to unfold that was so fascinating that he was compelled to dig into the matter further. He produced a one hour radio special on the subject and was deluged with mail and telephone calls from excited listeners. Next came requests for speaking engagements throughout Western Massachusetts. In January 1969 Mr. Spencer was the guest of a local television personality

(Tom Colton) and discussed the "Limbo of the Lost" for one hour live. After the program listeners, bookstores and libraries began asking him for a book.

Mr. Spencer says that the authors whose theories he read fall into one of two catagories. They are either careless gatherers of facts or outright falsifiers of the truth. This book is a report of only documented case histories of mysterious happenings in the Atlantic Ocean. It was written through demand as a labor of love.

John Wallace Spencer was born in Boston, Massachusetts, in 1934. He married Barbara Phillips in England. Their children are: Sherry Susan, John Wallace III and Geoffrey Phillip (twins).

LIMBO OF THE LOST

More than a thousand people and over a hundred ships and planes have mysteriously disappeared in an area of the Atlantic Ocean that I call the "Limbo of the Lost." Ghostly derelicts have been found floundering there, without a clue as to the whereabouts of the crews and passengers.

Tragedies connected to this region continually occur without explanation, without pattern, without warning and without reason. Extensive air-sea searches have been conducted without the satisfaction of finding enough evidence leading to a realistic answer. The few clues uncovered only add to the mysteries.

The area in question is not desolate, on the contrary it is bounded on the west and north by the eastern seaboard of North America; on the east by the Azores and other scattered islands, and on the south by Cuba . . . Jamaica . . . Haiti . . . Dominican Republic . . . Puerto Rico and the West Indies. Within its confines is Bermuda's 360 islands, The Bahamas' 20 inhabited islands, Nassau, Great Abaco, Andros Island plus hundreds of smaller islands too numerous to mention.

Air and sea lanes in the "Limbo" are in constant use both day and night by military, commercial and private aircraft, ships and boats. Because sea distances are relatively short, it is safe to surmise that the waters of the "Limbo of the Lost" are virtually covered by craft of one form or another.

Many titles have been hung on this deadly portion of the Mid-Atlantic Ocean: "Bermuda Triangle" (writer - Vincent H. Gaddis), "The Hoodoo Sea" (writer - John Godwin), "Triangle of Death" . . . "Triangle of Tragedy" . . . "Pentagon of Death" . . . "Port of the Missing."

JAPAN'S SEA OF TRAGEDY

Several other areas exist throughout the world where an unusually large number of unexplainable sea mysteries happen. The most famous is a region located southeast of Japan in the Pacific Ocean. Ships and boats have been disappearing in that area for more than a century, and in the early 1950's almost a dozen large ships vanished without leaving a trace to tell their tragic tales.

Since 1955 seamen have been avoiding this region. Scientists have stated that the previous mishaps theoretically could have been caused by volcanic explosions catching ships unexpectedly in their eruptions. This theory is fine but the question that is constantly being asked, not only of the Pacific area but also of the "Limbo of the Lost" is: "Why no debris, survivors, bodies, lifeboats or oil slicks?"

The major difference between other mysterious sea regions of the world and the "Limbo" zone is that not only are ships engulfed but aircraft as well disappear far beyond the laws of chance.

Nobody has ever proclaimed the "Limbo of the Lost" an official danger zone or is anybody apt to. What would happen to the tourist trade?

In spite of radar, radio, modern search technology, life saving apparatus and speed, man and his machines have and will continue to disappear. Whatever hovers over the "Limbo of the Lost" is responsible for the stranger-than-fiction stories of this book.

CONTENTS

CONTENTS

CHAPTER I

*UNITED STATES NAVY
HIT HARDEST WITH THE
DISAPPEARANCE OF NINE PLANES
AND NINETY-TWO PEOPLE*

LOST TRAINING MISSION
WEDNESDAY, DECEMBER 5, 1945

Getting ready for take-off from the runway of Fort Lauderdale, U. S. Air Naval Station, Florida were five Navy Grumman, TBM-3 Avenger Torpedo Bombers.

The World War II sea combat designed aircraft normally carried a crew of three. However, one crewman scheduled for the mission was unable to report for duty on that ill-fated day.

Each pilot went through his own pre-flight check:

Fuel - maximum 18,250 pounds (enough for over one-thousand miles).

Instruments and compass - check.

Radio - checked with tower and command pilot.

Life saving equipment - Mae West and self-inflating life raft - check.

At two o'clock, right on schedule, the five TBM's took off, assumed flight formation and headed out to sea toward the Bahamas. Several routine position reports were received but then at 5:25 p.m. (EST) a distress message from the mission's Flight Leader puzzled control tower officials:

"We seem to be lost . . . Have enough fuel for 75

more minutes . . . Can't tell whether over Atlantic or Gulf . . . Not sure but think we are 75 miles northeast of the Banana Naval Air Station," (located about two-hundred miles northeast of Miami). These were the last words received.

From the tempo of the conversation the control tower personnel at Fort Lauderdale got the impression the flight was caught in a blinding storm, but why couldn't they resume radio contact with any of the five planes?

AIR-SEA RESCUE MISSION LAUNCHED

As the last report was received from the TBM's, Commander Howard S. Roberts, Executive Officer of the Station, was in the tower. He immediately signaled air-sea rescue and within minutes a huge Martin Mariner (PBM) flying boat lumbered into the air fully equipped for rescue duty with a trained crew of thirteen.

According to officials, there was nothing to be overly concerned about because Avengers were known to have a high degree of buoyancy. "When other TBM's were downed at sea the crews were able to launch their life-rafts without even getting their feet wet."

Fort Lauderdale kept in constant contact with the rescue PBM. At approximately 7:30 p.m. the tower reported it was unable to raise the flying boat by radio.

Throughout the night the Coast Guard patrolled the seas while Navy planes scoured an area 275 miles northeast of Miami.

FULL SCALE SEARCH UNDERWAY

Navy officials reported that the baby flat-top, U. S. S. Solomons, an escort aircraft carrier, located off the southwest Florida coast had launched her thirty fighter planes into the search. Every plane available from the British Royal Air Force base at Wind Wor Field in the Bahamas was in the sky. Third Air Force stationed at Tampa was aloft and the Air Transport Command from Miami joined in flying low over the Everglades and the flat Florida land. All available patrol and merchant vessels in Florida waters had also joined in the hunt. In all, 252 Navy planes, hundreds of Army and Coast Guard planes and a fleet of surface craft were 150 miles out in the Atlantic from north of Jacksonville to the Bahamas.

CLUES RECEIVED

Naval officials admitted they had nothing new to report Thursday morning but they added that hope had not yet been abandoned. The great search armada was joined by a large "Dumbo" flying boat, equipped with a detachable lifeboat. The Destroyer Tender "Shenandoah" and the Coast Guard Cutter "Pandora" moved into the extended area 350 miles out on a line reaching from Palm Beach to St. Augustine. All at once, as if a tap was turned on, a flurry of conflicting reports were received from the search task force.

16

Explosion in the air:

Merchant Ship "Gaines Mills," reported that its crew had seen an explosion in the air and what appeared to be an airplane spin down into the ocean at approximately 7:50 Wednesday night. The vessel's Captain was unable to give the exact location, but at the time of the reported incident the "Gaines Mills" was off the coast of New Smyrna Beach, Florida.

Dozens of planes and surface craft were dispatched to the reported area, but no wreckage, oil or other clues were found. The aerial hunt was then farther extended 200 miles out to sea in a 400 mile front down the Florida coast from Jacksonville in the north to Miami in the south.

Red flares seen in Florida wilderness:

The three day old hunt for the lost fliers was suddenly intensified when an Eastern Airlines pilot, Captain J. D. Morrison reported to the Navy that he saw red flares and flashing lights "in the middle of a swamp" at about two o'clock Saturday morning, ten miles southwest of Melbourne, Florida. Captain Morrison, piloting a northbound passenger plane, was quoted as saying he saw human figures standing in the light of the flares but could not discern any wreckage. "I'm sure they were flares, not a fire," he said.

Five minutes after his first communique Captain Morrison reported he saw a fire burning in the dismal, sparsely populated region some twenty miles north of the spot where he had seen the flares.

A Navy plane was dispatched from the Banana River Naval Air Station. At 2:30 a.m. the pilot radioed that he also observed a flare about fifty miles inland.

At dawn a dense fog limited the visibility of aerial searchers to almost zero. The main hope of a rescue was centered on a small land army of wartime assault craft, weasels, marsh buggies, alligators and jeeps that groped their way through the bleak swamplands of North Central Florida. Throughout the day shuttling sweeps of Army, Navy and Coast Guard planes plus a Navy blimp from Lakehurst, New Jersey flew over the wild, desolate region. A helicopter also made a number of landings and sent men out to comb the marsh on foot in an attempt to locate wreckage or survivors.

Commander H. H. J. Benson of the U. S. 7th Naval District said, "We don't want to get any hopes too high, but I would like to report that we are moving everything up there to find those men if they are alive." He went on to say the hunt was being pressed with all available forces and disclosed that farmers in the Melbourne-Orlando area reported hearing an explosion on the night the six planes vanished. Commander Benson was quoted as saying, "This is the first time a whole flight of planes ever disappeared without a trace."

Two men on life rafts:

A pilot of an Army Air Corps plane reported seeing two men aboard two life rafts. He stated that the men waved as he flew toward their rafts but when he made his run over their crafts he could no longer see the men.

A Naval spokesman cast doubt on the report by saying that two survivors, no matter how exhausted, would never collapse simultaneously with rescue so near at hand after seeing a plane. The Navy's position was supported when the alleged rafts were found to be nothing more than packing cases bobbing in the waters some 300 miles due east of Melbourne.

Survivors rescued:

Hope again was raised when a report was received that stated two survivors had been rescued at sea by the tanker, "Erwin Russell." This too turned out to be erroneous. The Navy said the tanker's original report in effect read, "Lowering life boats to pick up survivors from raft." Subsequently the tanker radioed air-sea rescue headquarters in Miami stating they had made a mistake, instead of survivors or life raft, it had only found a tow-target used by the Navy for gunnery practice at sea.

Two more men on rafts reported:

A report was received from the Army Air Field at Boca Raton that stated, the pilot, co-pilot and nine crewmen of an Army B-24 found two life rafts close together in an area 290 miles east of Melbourne. They were almost sure they saw two men huddled in one of the rafts.

The pilot, Leonard Bostick, and his co-pilot Eugene B. Hollander were quoted as saying they flew over the rafts for about four and a half hours before a failing gas supply compelled them to return to base. Here is an extract from their official report: "At 10:45 a.m. (EST) we located rafts and circled over them. While circling we saw two one-man rafts apparently tied together. At the beginning every man in the crew believed there were two men in the rafts. However, as the day wore on we could not be sure." Bostick related how they flew down to an altitude of several hundred feet but heavy winds prevented them from going lower for closer observation. He said they tried to direct surface vessels to the rafts but no contacts were made by the time they were forced to leave the scene.

An extensive air-sea search was conducted in and around the reported area but again without success.

Parachute spotted:

The Coast Guard cutter, "The Vigalante" reported sighting "something which could have been a parachute," 180 miles east of Melbourne. Later the cutter, radioed that it had scoured the particular area without locating anything that might be remotely considered a clue.

HOPE FADING

Only sixty-six planes took to the skies at dawn on December 10th. Most of the aircraft, a number of merchant ships and one destroyer-tender had been released from further search operations.

Naval officials announced that the air-sea rescue operation would be called off at dusk unless new evidence could be discovered. They expressed fear of ever finding any of the fliers alive, but added, "we have not given up yet, if those men are still alive we'll do everything to find them."

Search craft carried out orders of the last day of the quest by combing 25,000 square miles, yard by yard for even a slight clue. As darkness blacked out the sea, the Navy disclosed that 930 air sorties and many searches by thirty ships were made in the futile five day hunt. Every possibility had been explored before the search was discontinued. 380,000 square miles of sea, coast, land and swamps were combed without uncovering a single shred of evidence that any of the 27 fliers were still alive. Navy officials stressed that planes and surface craft which travel the area where the airmen are believed to have disappeared would remain on the alert indefinitely.

SPECULATION

All six planes experienced engine trouble:

The possibility that all six planes experienced engine trouble and crashed without leaving a trace is too farfetched to bear any weight.

Mass air collision or freak water spout plucked planes out of sky:

These theories would account for the abrupt interruption of radio contact. Certainly a tremendous amount of debris, a gigantic oil slick and several bodies would have remained to tell the tale. What about the Martin Mariner flying boat, could it have met the same fate?

Magnetic disturbance affecting all compasses causing planes to fly in circles until fuel was exhausted:

According to Coast Guard officials no reports were ever filed pertaining to magnetic disturbances in the area of the "Limbo of the Lost." If the planes ran into a magnetic storm that affected their compasses, they would not fly in circles but would have set a bearing on the sun setting above the western horizon. If the planes ran out of fuel for one reason or another all of the crew were trained in ditching procedures and could exist for many days in the open sea.

Unknown type of atmospheric aberation swallowed all the planes:

Officially, the Navy said the theory of a "hole in the sky" did not exist nor had one existed in the past.

Adverse weather conditions:

The U. S. Weather Bureau in Miami reported freak winds, attended by gusts of forty miles per hour or higher, as well as showers and thunderstorms prevailed over the area off the Banana River Station at the time when the last message was received from the Avengers.

A Navy spokesman explained that the gusts were not strong enough to blow the TBM's off their course.

BOARD OF INQUIRY BAFFLED

A Navy Department statement declared that a

combat training Flight Leader was in charge of the Avenger's group and that all of the crew members involved in the flight were experienced from slightly over one to over six years. They discounted the possibility that the planes might have developed flight trouble and landed at other fields, pointing out that if that had happened their home base would have been notified immediately.

The Naval Board of Inquiry concluded its investigation without the advantage of having a trace of real evidence to work with. They listened to testimony of witnesses and studied the few facts available. The Board expressed complete bafflement that all six planes could just simply disappear without leaving a trace or clue. A Board officer was quoted as saying, "This unprecedented peacetime loss seems to be a total mystery, the strangest ever investigated in the annals of Naval aviation." To this day no logical solution to the disappearances has ever been found.

For personal interview and partial list of those lost, consult Appendix A.

NAVY PLANE WITH 42 MISSING
SATURDAY, OCTOBER 30, 1954

Forty-two people including four women and five children took off in a four-engine Navy Super-Constellation from Patuxent River Naval Air Station, Maryland. After two and a half hours of flying, the pilot reported that he would have to return to Patuxent Station because of mechanical trouble.

When they landed another Super-Constellation was pressed into service and at 9:39 p.m., Saturday, October 30, 1954, the 42 people were back in the air. Next stop was scheduled for Lagens, the Azores and then on to Port Lyautey, Africa.

At 11:00 p.m. a routine position report was received placing the triple-tailed transport at a point more than 350 miles off the Maryland coast. That was the last word to be heard from the military passenger plane.

HUNT STARTED

Air-sea search operations got underway at 1:00 a.m. after the four-engine plane failed to make two scheduled, hourly contacts with shore.

Joining the hunt were planes and ships from up and down the eastern seaboard, Bermuda, the Azores and the Mediterranean. Also included in the search were aircraft carriers and destroyers.

Search conditions were reported as generally favorable. It was partly cloudy with light winds in the ribbon of ocean area where the hunt was conducted. The Weather Bureau in New York reported that the water temperatures along the search route ranged from the mid-fifties up.

Planes and ships with special radar for night operations pressed on with the search. The Navy said the plane was equipped with five, twenty-man life rafts, 102 life vests, ninety exposure suits, emergency radio and a signal pistol with twelve shells.

In operational command of the search was Vice Admiral Laurence T. DuBose, Commander of the Eastern Sea Frontier. His office reported that about 200 planes and thirty surface vessels, including the aircraft carrier Leyte, were concentrated in a 120-mile path that stretched from the Maryland coast to the Azores.

A B-29 rescue plane flew from Prestwick, Scotland, to join in the hunt. Slung under its fuselage was a completely equipped fifteen-man life raft that could be dropped into the ocean from an altitude of 800 feet and be guided by remote control to any survivors who might be sighted.

The missing Super-Constellation had enough fuel on board to stay in the air until 10 a.m., October 31st. Flying time to the Azores ordinarily took about nine hours. There was hope that the pilot somehow managed to ditch safely and that survivors had time to climb onto life rafts.

Planes and ships crisscrossed and recrossed the area in a scientific pattern that covered about 1-million square miles. Every yard of the search area was scanned by sight and radar every six hours.

Numerous reports of debris, oil and a faint SOS were received. Captain Ray Needham, Naval rescue co-ordinator for the area said that all reports received were checked-out but there had been "no valid sightings."

NAVY ENDS HUNT

At 3:00 p.m., Wednesday, November 3rd the Navy gave orders to abandon the search for the Super-Constellation. Vice Admiral DuBose informed reporters, "The search was called off because of extreme weather conditions."

SEARCH FOR NAVY PLANE RENEWED

The search for the missing Super-Constellation was suddenly renewed on November 6th in the hope of finding some physical clue to the cause of the tragedy.

No life rafts nor bodies nor debris were ever found. Once again another plane flew into the "Limbo of the Lost."

For the names of the crew and passengers that were lost, consult Appendix B.

NAVY SEAPLANE HUNTED
FRIDAY, NOVEMBER 9, 1956

A U. S. Navy, Martin "Marlin" P5M, twin-engined patrol flying boat with seven enlisted men and three officers aboard was reported as missing Friday night, November 9, 1956. The plane, assigned to Squadron "49" - Naval Station in Bermuda, radioed a last position report at 8:30 p.m. as 350 miles north of its home station.

When the Martin's next position reports were not received a search by air and sea craft was ordered, but without any great haste; after all the missing craft was a seaplane and if anything had happened to its engines the pilot would just simply sit down on the sea and await rescue. According to officials the aircraft had enough fuel to have stayed aloft until 6:30 in the morning.

Then a message from the Liberian freighter "The Captain Lyras" changed the whole tempo of the hunt. She reported, seeing a plane in flames over the Atlantic Ocean at a point about 400 miles east-southeast of New York City at 9:15 p.m.

Coast Guard aircraft from Quonset Point, Rhode Island and Floyd Bennett Field, Brooklyn; four other P5M's stationed in Bermuda, two P2V Neptune patrol bombers from Maryland, plus two Navy destroyers and the Coast Guard Cutter "Chincoteague" proceeded to the area given by "The Captain Lyras." At the time the "Chincoteague" was alerted she was 180 miles from "The Captain Lyras" on her way to Norfolk, Virginia with thirty-three men from the German freighter "Helga Bolten." They were rescued from the 10,000 dead-weight-ton vessel which developed trouble some 400 miles off Newfoundland.

Shortly after the initial report of the sighting of the burning aircraft "The Captain Lyras" radioed that it had seen what appeared to be a life raft with a light on it about four miles away. However, it lost sight of it in the darkness. The freighter reported that she would stand by with all the crew looking out.

As the first aircraft and cutter arrived at the scene flares were dropped and a quick search was conducted, yet no wreckage or life rafts were sighted.

The aviation weather forecast at the New York International Airport, Idlewild, Queens said that a cold front was in the vicinity which was about 380 miles north-northwest of Bermuda with winds about 33 miles per hour. Navy craft at the search area reported scattered clouds at 1,000 feet, showers with good visibility and moderate seas. If anything was out there they would find it.

Meanwhile the joint sea-air search was placed under the coordination of the Navy's Eastern Sea Frontier Command in New York. The Commandant, Vice Admiral Frederick W. McMahon, was quoted as declaring the Navy plane "may or may not" be the alleged sighted burning craft. A check by the Coast Guard, the Military Air Transport Service and the Civil Aeronautics Adminstration's communications center revealed that no other planes had been reported missing or in trouble.

The mystery became even more clouded when the Coast Guard reported that a ship in the vicinity of "The Captain Lyras" released information about seeing a plane flying overhead and had flashed a large spotlight on it, however the plane was not in trouble. There was a good possibility that the light on the plane might have been seen by "The Captain Lyras" and mistaken for flames.

Again hope was raised as Naval aircraft and surface ships were dispatched to a point 300 miles northwest of Bermuda after the Spanish freighter "Astro" reported sighting a white flare in the area at six o'clock, Sunday night. Nothing was found.

SEARCH CALLED OFF

The Navy and Coast Guard air and surface craft continued their search between Bermuda and Rhode Island, day and night until Tuesday, November 13th when the hunt was officially called off.

Another craft with its entire crew entered into the oblivion of the "Limbo of the Lost" without giving its hunters a radio signal or a visible clue to work on.

For the names of those lost, consult Appendix C.

NAVY PLANE AND 15 FLIERS LOST
WEDNESDAY, JULY 18, 1945

Less than five months before the five TBM patrol planes disappeared another Navy plane had vanished. Every air-sea rescue unit in South Florida and the Royal Air Force from the Bahamas had been mobilized to hunt for a missing PB-4YW, four engined, Privateer with four officers and eleven enlisted men on board.

Lieutenant William C. Bailey of New York piloted the big plane off the runway of Miami Naval Air Station on a routine training mission. The single-tailed version of the Army's B-24 headed out to sea at 12:26, Wednesday morning, July 18, 1945, and never returned.

Once again another gigantic but futile air-sea search was conducted without turning up anything, either in the sea or on the beaches. It was as though a small dress rehearsal had been conducted by whatever lurks in the "Limbo of the Lost."

CHAPTER II

EIGHTY PEOPLE DISAPPEAR ON AIRLINERS IN TWELVE MONTHS

MYSTERIOUS DISAPPEARANCE
OF THE STAR TIGER
FRIDAY, JANUARY 30, 1948

As the world received word that Orville Wright, co-inventor of the airplane died, one of the greatest peacetime air-sea searches ever conducted was being carried out in the Atlantic northeast of Bermuda. A desperate attempt was underway to find twenty-five passengers and six crewmen reported missing along with their British South American Airways, four-engine, Avro, Tudor IV, luxury airliner, "Star Tiger."

The thirty-two-passenger plane, on a flight from London to Havana, was on its third stage from Santa Maria in the Azores to Hamilton, Bermuda, a distance of 1,960 miles.

A radio message sent by the "Star Tiger's" pilot, Captain David Colby at 10:30, Thursday night, January 29th established that he would reach Hamilton at approximately 1:00 a.m. (EST) an hour and a half late.

At about 1:00 a.m. Captain Colby radioed, "Still approximately 440 miles northeast of Bermuda and bucking strong headwinds." That was the last message heard from the "Star Tiger."

When the Tudor IV was reported overdue, Hamilton

32

tower tried to establish radio contact without success. Air-sea rescue headquarters was alerted. It was estimated the Avro had enough fuel to last until approximately 3:15 a.m.

DOWNED CRAFT COULD FLOAT

Captain Leslie S. Cruthirds, at search headquarters said, the main hope of the rescue units was that the "Star Tiger's" pilot was able to ditch the huge plane without seriously damaging the fuselage. The Tudor IV, similar to the U. S. Air Force C-54, is sufficiently pressurized and hermetically sealed that, if undamaged, would allow everyone aboard to get set free in the rubber life rafts she carried.

The temperature of the water in the search area was about 65 degrees, meaning that there was a good chance for those who managed to get aboard a raft. Each life raft was equipped with a survival kit which included a "Gibson Girl," a small hand-cranked radio designed to be held between the knees. It operated on the 500 kilocycles band and the range was generally limited to a radius of fifty to a few hundred miles, depending upon the kind of antenna used.

SEA SEARCH UNDERWAY

Direction of the search operations was assigned to Colonel Thomas D. Ferguson, Commander of the United States Air Force Base in Bermuda.

Two USAF Flying Fortresses from Bermuda's Kindley Field and another from MacDill Field, Florida were the first search craft underway. The B-17's carried the latest lifeboats designed to be dropped by parachute. Also two B-25 bombers and a C-47 transport from Mitchell Field, New York were assigned the area from Ocean City, New Jersey north to Long Island, and eastward out over the Atlantic for 500 miles. All aircraft were equipped with several life rafts. Six other planes at Mitchell Field were placed on standby alert.

The Coast Guard aired three PBY amphibian airplanes plus three cutters, the "Mendota" from Wilmington, North Carolina, the "Cherokee" from Norfolk, Virginia and the "Androscoggin" from New York. The cutters were dispatched by Eastern Area Search and Rescue Headquarters of the Coast Guard in New York.

Two commercial steamers and a British South American Airways plane were sent out to work over a large area 300 to 400 miles northeast and east of Bermuda.

The Air Transport Command (ATC) announced that fourteen of its planes had joined the search. A spokesman for ATC in Washington, D. C. said the planes would continue the hunt and that others would be added if the "Star Tiger" was not found in the meantime. A C-54, Transport of ATC bound from the Azores to the United States and a B-17 Flying Fortress in which Major General William E. Hall was flying to Germany were pressed into the hunt when they landed at Bermuda.

Six 4-engine transports of Pan American World Airways flying the New York to San Juan, Puerto Rico, route were ordered to leave their usual course and swing over the area in which it was believed the Tudor IV was lost. However, rain squalls and limited visibility made searching difficult.

Search planes became airborne from bases as far north as Stephensville, Newfoundland, to as far south as Borninquen Air Force Base, San Juan. Planes were dispatched or alerted from every base along the Atlantic coast.

The Coast Guard had three speedy sea-going motor launches 30, 60 and 105 feet long at Hamilton on standby with orders to put to sea at once if life rafts were located.

Desk officers and ground crews at Kindley Field volunteered to go aloft in B-29's attached to the Weather Reconnaissance Squadron, and in other planes as observers so that all flight trained officers and enlisted men could be assigned to flight operations duties.

ADVERSE WEATHER HAMPERS SEARCH

As the sun went down on the first day of the big hunt, Colonel Ferguson at search command headquarters reported that all his planes had been grounded because of adverse weather conditions. The hunt would continue at dawn unless adverse weather conditions again balked their efforts.

One of the search pilots said, "I doubt anyone could survive in seas like that." Other search pilots reported seas were very stormy with waves of up to 40 feet high.

CLUES FOUND

Low flying plane:

Part of the search fleet was diverted, for a time, to a position northwest of Bermuda when Captain W. R. Richards, Eastern Area Chief of Staff of the Coast Guard received a report sent by the 5,800-ton, "S. S. Troubador."

The message said, "sighted low-flying plane with lights blinking at 2:10 a.m. (EST) halfway between Bermuda and the Delaware Bay entrance." Captain Richards said it was possible the plane could have overshot Bermuda because of a squall that hit the island at about the time the plane was due there.

Later it was learned that the reported craft was a Pan-American Airways plane and definitely not in trouble.

Debris sighted by B-17:

The Coast Guard sent surface cutters to an area between Bermuda and Cape Hatteras, North Carolina because of a report sent by the pilot of a B-17 out of Westover Field, Massachusetts. The pilot said he spotted what was believed to be a cylindrical object plus yellow and black boxes floating nearby.

When the cutters, "Cherokee," "Androscoggin" and the Coast Guard tug "Acushnet," reached the area they reported finding only a roll of sheet cork that from the air could look like a cylinder, but no sign of the other reported objects, only rough seas, lowering skies and winds of near gale force.

Oil slicks:

Captain W. M. Hackett, pilot of a search plane, reported oil slicks 240 miles northwest of Bermuda.

Another pilot reported sighting oil patches 500 miles east-northeast of Bermuda.

Still another pilot reported spotting an oil slick between 75 and 100 miles northeast of Bermuda.

A search of all reported areas showed no trace of the missing plane. Search and Rescue Headquarters of the Coast Guard in New York pointed out that the slicks described most probably were caused by bilge pumping from passing steamers.

Flares and raft sighted:

Two Pan American Airways planes reported flares and a raft to the south of Bermuda.

The flares were never confirmed but the tanker "Esso Philadelphia," called to the scene, reported, the raft found was launched from a surface vessel and it had been in the water a long time.

INQUIRY SCHEDULE IN LOSS OF STAR TIGER

On Monday, February 2nd, G. S. Lindgren, parliamentary secretary of the British Ministry of Civil Aviation announced to the House of Commons that a public inquiry would be made into the loss of the Tudor IV airliner "Star Tiger." He said the Ministry would seek technical advice from the Air Registration Board and all Tudor IV's had been withdrawn from service.

A spokesman for the British South American Airways Corporation said his company knew no reason why the Air Registration Board should not assure the Ministry of Civil Aviation of the airworthiness of the Tudor IV. As soon as this assurance had been received use of the aircraft would certainly be resumed.

The airline had been operating three Tudor IV's on the Bermuda route, the first of which came into service in October 1947.

Officials of the British Overseas Airways Corporation (BOAC), also uses Tudor IV's but they said the grounding would not affect the company's overall operation.

SEARCH CONTINUES FROM BERMUDA

All available planes at Bermuda were ordered to continue the search. Forty aircraft flew over 200,000 square miles of ocean on overlapping courses. Although the air and surface hunt was being continued, hope was fading rapidly and it was feared that all aboard the "Star Tiger" were lost.

FAINT RADIO SIGNALS REVIVE SEARCH

Amateur and professional radio operators from Halifax to Miami reported picking up several radio messages in code that spelled out the name "Tiger." Others reported hearing "Star Tiger" spelled out. The code messages were picked up on an international channel for voice communication in an emergency, however, voice was not used.

Navy and Canadian Air Force officers in Halifax reported the signals were of an improvised code nature in which someone laboriously tapped out one dot for "A" two dots for "B" and so on through the alphabet.

The signals were heard late Tuesday night, February 3rd and were not picked up during the day. All Navy, Coast Guard, aviation and shipping radios from Canada to South America listened for the signals to resume.

The Federal Communications Commission sent out sensitive mobile direction finding units in an effort to pick up the signals and triangulate their position. If such a fix could have been made from three points the location of the sender would be approximated.

Search officials emphatically denied that the downed plane could have survived this long in the water or that any of the "Star Tiger's" heavy radio gear could possibly have been put on a raft. If anybody was still alive why didn't they use the light "Gibson Girl" transmitter provided for just such an emergency?

In any event forty aircraft at Kindley Field and various other fields along the southern coast were standing by. Coast Guard cutters remained waiting in the areas where wreckage and oil slicks were reported.

No further signals were heard. The only logical explanation was that some person or persons with a twisted mind sent the messages as a prank.

British Ministry of Civil Aviation announced in

London, that it was "presumed" the plane and its passengers and crew had been lost at sea.

AIR MINISTRY REPORTS LOSS UNEXPLAINED

On September 28, 1948, the verdict of the court appointed by the Minister of Civil Aviation to investigate the disappearance of the "Star Tiger" was published as a White Paper (Cmd. 7517, Stationery Office, 2s.).

The fate of the "Star Tiger," the British South American Airways liner, must remain an unsolved mystery. "It may truly be said that no more baffling problem has ever been presented for investigation."

There were no grounds to suppose that the design of the Tudor IV aircraft caused the mishap. No evidence existed leading to possible technical errors or omissions. The possibility that fire broke out, a disasterous mechanical breakdown or any part of the plane's power plant causing the disappearance is remote and most improbable.

The final paragraph of the report reads: "In the complete absence of any reliable evidence as to either the nature or the cause of the disaster to the "Star Tiger," the court has not been able to do more than suggest possibilities, none of which reaches the level even of probability. What happened in this case will never be known."

For the names and information about those lost on the "Star Tiger," consult Appendix D.

DC-3 WITH THIRTY PERSONS DOWN AT SEA
TUESDAY, DECEMBER 28, 1948

Twenty-seven passengers including two babies boarded a chartered twin-engine, DC-3A airliner at San Juan Airport. Most of the passengers were Puerto Ricans returning to New York from a holiday excursion visit to their homeland for Christmas.

The pilot, Captain Robert Linquist of Ft. Myers, Florida filed his instrument flight plan, designating departure, San Juan - destination New York with a stop over scheduled for Miami, estimated time of arrival - 4:30 a.m. (EST).

The co-pilot, Ernie E. Hill, Jr., 22, of Miami, completed the pre-flight check as the stewardess, Mary Burke of Jersey City, New Jersey checked off the passenger list.

At 10:30 p.m., December 27th with everything in order for the long 1,200 mile flight, the big plane, loaded to capacity, took off into the dark clear skies of the West Indies.

A position report was received by the Airways Radio Station at Kingston, Jamaica shortly after 1:00 a.m.

At 4:13 a.m. the Civil Aeronautics Overseas Radio at New Orleans, Louisiana picked up a faint position report in which Captain Linquist stated his position as "Fifty miles South of Miami."

This would place the DC-3 well within sight of land. The Overseas Radio repeated the position to the plane and asked confirmation.

There was no answer. Repeated calls brought no response. An alert was sounded and other stations attempted to reach the aircraft by radio, without results.

The DC-3 was owned by Karl Knight, of Miami, but had been leased to Airborne Transport, Incorporated of New York. Mr. Knight said he had nothing to do with the operation of the leased craft. He learned it was missing when, landing another plane, he heard Airways Radio making urgent requests to the silent charter flight to respond to messages.

VAST SEARCH ON FOR MISSING PLANE

Air-sea rescue was alerted for fear the big plane had crashed in the area of the Florida Keys and an immediate air and surface hunt was launched. The coastal waters in the region of the Keys is so clear and shallow that the DC-3, if there, could have been easily seen on the bottom.

At dawn when search craft reported finding nothing in the vicinity of the Keys, a fleet of forty-three airplanes of the Army, Navy and Coast Guard from Florida and the Caribbean began the far flung patrol spreading over the Florida straits, northern Cuba, Bahama Islands and the air route from Miami to San

Juan. The search was later extended to the entire Florida peninsula, Charleston, South Carolina, the east end of Cuba and the eastern Gulf of Mexico. At nightfall a Navy blimp joined the hunt.

A Coast Guard officer said the DC-3's fuel would have been used up by about 5:45 a.m. He pointed out that the plane was fully equipped with survival gear including a "Gibson Girl" emergency radio, life rafts and individual life preservers.

Gusty weather hampered the widespread search somewhat, but Coast Guard officials said there were few cancellations among the vast fleet of aircraft and ships combing the seas.

SURVIVOR REPORTS RECEIVED

A report was received by a ship that it had sighted flares in the area of the Bahamas.

Seven Air Force planes were dispatched into the region and a thorough search was conducted, but like before the results were negative.

* * * * * *

Two air-sea rescue planes spotted the remains of a badly burned plane on Andros Island in the Bahamas.

A land party was flown to the scene. The mystery of the missing DC-3 continued when the land group reported the wreckage was that of an old wartime plane known to have crashed many years before.

* * * * * *

An unconfirmed report was received at the Coast Guard's air-sea rescue headquarters that survivors were sighted on a beach in Cuba. A spokesman said, "The information did not even designate on which side of the island the survivors were believed sighted, but we plan to scour every inch of coastline, if necessary, in the hope that we may sight something." He emphasized that the report was entirely unofficial. If nothing was found on the east end of Cuba the Coast Guard official said they would extend the search to the south side of Cuba.

Military aircraft in the vicinity were diverted to Cuba's coastline on the offchance that the rumor was correct. A complete sweep proved the lead unfounded.

SEARCH ABANDONED

At dusk, Monday, January 10th, the Coast Guard announced that all clues leading to the whereabouts of the DC-3 charter flight had been exhausted.

Several-hundred-thousand square miles of sea, coast and land had been scanned from the Caribbean and Gulf, to the Keys and Everglades without turning up debris, bodies or even an oil slick.

Not so much as a trace remained as to the fate of the thirty persons who flew into the unknown moments of the "Limbo of the Lost."

For the published list of those that vanished, consult Appendix E.

ANOTHER BRITISH
SOUTH AMERICAN AIRWAYS PLANE GONE
MONDAY, JANUARY 17, 1949

Catastrophe once again struck the British South American Airways Corporation just thirteen-days short of one year since the disappearance of their airliner "Star Tiger." This time it was her sister aircraft "Star Ariel" that vanished.

The four-engine Tudor IV passenger plane departed Bermuda on a six-hour, 1000 mile flight to Kingston, Jamaica at 7:42 a.m. (EST), Monday, January 17, 1949. It was the second leg of her flight from London Airport to Santiago, Chile, estimated time of arrival scheduled for 1:42 p.m.

Captain J. C. McPhee, the "Ariel's" pilot radioed Bermuda Radio Control at 8:50 a.m. that he was changing frequency to make contact with Jamaica Control. By 10:10 a.m. BSAA officials at Jamaica had tried to establish contact with the big passenger plane without success. Two hours and twenty-eight minutes after the last radio report was received an air-sea rescue alert was sounded.

Bermuda authorities said, Captain McPhee's plane had enough gasoline for ten-hours of flying. Although the

"Ariel" was only carrying 13 passengers and a crew of six she had a seating capacity of thirty-two. Her full designation was Avro, Tudor IV, Post War, pressurized cabin Luxury Airliner. The Tudor IV had five emergency exits, carried three large dinghies, one fitted with a radio transmitter, and lifebelts were stowed under the passenger seats and in the crew's compartment.

GREAT SEA HUNT PLANNED

With the "Star Ariel's" fuel tanks evidently drained at 5:42 p.m., and the plane still missing, the Coast Guard marshalled its forces and formed plans for an extensive search to begin at dawn. Meanwhile, just before dusk, a U. S. Army plane from Kindley Field, Bermuda made a sweep of the area of the Tudor's last reported position, without sighting anything. All ships and aircraft along the big plane's route and in the area of the western Caribbean were alerted by radio to keep a sharp lookout.

MacDill Field said a B-29 Superfortress was scheduled to take off at 3:00 a.m., and a B-17 at 5:00 a.m. The Coast Guard in New York relayed that rescue planes from Salem, Massachusetts, Brooklyn, New York and Elizabeth City, North Carolina would go to Bermuda and begin intensive flights over the search area at daybreak. Other planes from Florida Coast Guard bases and planes of the other services were alerted. Nassau reported aircraft would leave at dawn to search the eastern Bahamas. A U. S. Navy plane equipped with radar was set to go aloft from the Guantanamo base in Cuba. Aircraft carriers "Kearsarge" and "Leyte" and the battleship "Missouri" joined six U. S. destroyers thrown into the search from Jamaica.

SEARCH UNDERWAY

As the sun broke through the darkness, planes and ships began the tremendous task of looking for the proverbial "drop in the ocean." By high noon the Coast Guard announced that an estimated 72 search planes, many ships and approximately thirteen thousand men were actively engaged in the hunt for life.

As the days passed without finding a trace of the "Star Ariel" the U. S. Air Force added sixteen more planes, twelve B-29s, two Catalina flying boats and two B-17s from the United States with orders assigning them to Hamilton, Bermuda.

Pan American World Airways instructed pilots of two of its planes en-route from San Juan to Miami to change course and search the area. BSAA, operators of the "Ariel" ordered another Tudor IV, which left Nassau, Bahama to make the hunt. The entire personnel of the Cuban Armed Services were placed on search alert.

RESULTS OF SEARCH

Bermuda reported that planes flying in relays had scoured over 150-thousand square miles of ocean in an area roughly 125 to 500 miles to the south-southwest without finding any survivors, a trace of wreckage or even an oil slick. Spokesmen stressed the fact that not a single message denoting trouble of any kind had been received from the "Ariel" after she asked Bermuda Radio Control to transfer her to Jamaica Control about an hour after departure from Hamilton. As in the loss of the "Tiger", searchers also were mystified by the lack of any SOS distress message.

A British South American Airways Constellation pilot reported early in the morning of January 20th that he twice sighted lights on the water and then what his crew thought was a floating object reflected in the light of the moon.

The crew said the light was seen 300 miles south-southwest of Bermuda. An Air Force spokesman added that search craft had been out flying wing-tip to wing-tip, over the reported area, in both an upper and lower covering, but had not sighted anything. Search headquarters issued a statement that they held out little hope of developments.

Interest in the search increased during the afternoon of January 22nd when one of the hunt planes spotted a yellow object measuring five feet by four feet, presumably the same object previously reported.

Aerial investigation proved the reported sighting to be a large box that could not possibly be connected with the lost aircraft.

* * * * * *

The possibility that sabotage was responsible for the

disappearance was raised in London by Sir Roy Dobson managing director of A. V. Roe & Co., Ltd., makers of Tudor planes. This explanation was dismissed because most certainly a tremendous amount of debris would have been found.

Lord Pakenham, Minister of Civil Aviation, announced in the House of Lords that BSAA had temporarily grounded its Tudor IV's for a special examination.

The Tudor type aircraft had been the subject of considerable controversy in British Parliamentary and aviation circles since it went into operation four years prior to the "Star Ariel's" disappearance. Designed as a compromise airplane with the wings of the Royal Air Force Lancaster bomber and a roomy commercial fuselage, it had been successively redesigned and developed as Britain's principal competitor to American DC-4s and Constellations in transatlantic commercial aviation.

In December, 1948 it was announced that BSAA had received a full certificate of the airworthiness of Tudor IV's after extensive modifications to fuselage and engines.

HUNT FOR PLANE HALTED

After five days of covering the Atlantic search area section by section without turning up a single clue, the U. S. Air Force announced the hunt was abandoned as of January 22nd. According to spokesmen at Hamilton,

Bermuda, "It was necessary to give up the search because both planes and personnel were nearing the exhaustion point."

The "Star Ariel" was the second plane within the short period of one month to disappear without a trace in the "Limbo of the Lost." The other lost craft was a DC-3 airliner on a flight from San Juan to Miami. The hunt for her was called off, without finding a single clue, twelve days earlier on January 10, 1949.

RIDDLE UNSOLVED BY INQUIRY

The following information has been extracted from the report by the Chief Inspector of Accidents, Air Commodore Vernon Brown, which was published on December 20, 1949. (M.C.A.P. 78, H. M. Stationery Office, 3s net), states: "Through lack of evidence due to no wreckage having been found the cause of the accident to the "Star Ariel" is unknown."

The "Star Ariel," was lost almost exactly a year after a sister aircraft, the "Star Tiger," had disappeared in much the same area in equally mysterious circumstances."

"These two losses led to the withdrawal of the Tudor IV's for carrying passengers, and they have not been employed for this purpose by the corporation since, even though they have operated successfully on the Berlin air-lift and elsewhere."

In his report on the "Star Ariel," Air Commodore Brown stated there was no evidence of defect in, or failure of, any part of the aircraft or its equipment before its departure from Bermuda. The pilot was experienced on the route; the radio officer was very experienced and dependable and above average in being able to effect instrument repairs, and he also was experienced on this crossing; good radio communication had been maintained with the aircraft up to and including receipt of its last message; there were no weather complications, and a study of weather reports gives no reason to believe that the accident was due to meteorological conditions. There was also no evidence of sabotage.

It appeared the "Star Ariel" had joined her sister aircraft, "Star Tiger" and the DC-3 charter flight in the record book of unsolved mysteries of the "Limbo of the Lost."

For official list of missing, consult Appendix F.

B. S. A. A. FOOTNOTE

British South American Airways' main mission was divided between serving Bermuda, the West Indies and the west coast of South America.

Avro Lancastrians opened the B. S. A. A. route on September 2, 1946, and were replaced by the ill-fated Tudor IV's a year later on October 31st.

As I pointed out in the preceding story of the "Star Ariel" not only were the Tudor IV's withdrawn from service but this last disappearance without a satisfactory explanation was the straw that broke the airlines back.

The British mid-Atlantic service was not resumed until March 2, 1950 when BOAC (which by that time had taken over BSAA) opened a Constellation service via Bermuda.

In the interim a connection had been maintained by way of New York, Bermuda and Nassau, to Kingston, Panama and Lima, with British York transport planes based at Nassau. Constellations continued to provide the service, which was extended from Nassau to Santiago, Chile between October 1950 and May 1, 1951. Not until March 5, 1952 was the longer route via Gander, Newfoundland reintroduced. Then the Caribbean once again was reached as an extension of the main North Atlantic services.

CHAPTER III

TRUTH, FICTION
AND
DISASTER IN THE ATLANTIC

AIR - SEA RESCUE

When conducting a search definite "standard operating procedures" are closely followed by air-sea rescue personnel. Clues to the whereabouts or fate of the hunted can be quickly uncovered if the area of the last known approximate or projected position of a missing craft is searched thoroughly and quickly.

Search personnel are trained to spot floating debris, oil slicks, large schools of fish (shark or barracuda), life saving craft and floating bodies, dead or alive.

Under no circumstances will an evaluation of a possible clue be determined from a distance. Assistance must be called in for close-up analysis of a suspect target.

The following true case is an excellent example of how an air-sea rescue search is conducted:

TWO AF JET TANKERS FEARED LOST
WEDNESDAY, AUGUST 28, 1963

Two Strategic Air Command, KC-135A, Stratotankers roared off the runway of Homestead Air Force Base, south of Miami, on the morning of Wednesday,

August 28, 1963. The four engine jets, Air Force versions of Boeing's 707 passenger airliners, were scheduled for a routine aerial refueling mission between Bermuda and the Bahamas. The skies were clear, ideal flying weather for the delicate rendezvous job.

At noon the tankers contacted Homestead tower with a routine position report, approximately 300 miles southwest of Bermuda. When the big jets were reported as overdue and could not be contacted by radio, the all too familiar air-sea rescue alert was sounded.

The missing KC-135's had a range of 4,500 miles and a cruising speed of 600 miles per hour. According to projected figures they had enough fuel to stay in the air until approximately 6:00 p.m.

DEBRIS FOUND

Throughout the night searchers covered the region of the downed crafts' last known position. The next day, Thursday, August 29th one of the search planes, a C-54 out of Bermuda reported an oil slick about 350 miles southwest of Bermuda. A ship also reported finding a life jacket in the same vicinity.

Coast Guard search headquarters announced, after examining the reported items, that they definitely were not from the missing KC-135's.

* * * * * *

The merchant ship "Azalea City" out of Wilmington, Delaware, retrieved a flight helmet stenciled "Gardner" and other items including three rubber life rafts of the type carried by the tankers, several life jackets and an exposure suit. The Coast Guard cutter "Owasco" from New London, Connecticut, also picked up debris over a wide area in the same vicinity, 300 miles southwest of Bermuda.

Spokesmen at the Air Rescue Service Headquarters, Orlando, Florida said, that a ten square mile "floating junkyard" of debris was from at least one of the two missing tankers. No survivors were spotted, however, and the fate of the crewmen appeared dim.

* * * * * *

Two HU-16B Grumman Albatross Amphibian planes sighted a second concentration of wreckage Friday, August 30th, 160 miles from the "floating junkyard" of debris. The new find was 400 miles east of Fort Pierce, Florida, but sea conditions prevented the planes from landing.

Air Force officials said a Coast Guard cutter was en-route and if the debris was that of the second jet tanker it would appear to conflict with a theory that the jets had collided. They went on to say the latest discovery spurred new hope into the massive air-sea rescue search for possible survivors.

Shortly after the cutter arrived at the scene, air-sea command received a report that the debris was not of the missing KC-135. Nothing more than on old buoy in a patch of dark seaweed was found.

HUNT FOR TANKER JETS HALTED

After five days of scouring the Atlantic for survivors the Air Force gave up the search. They announced that wreckage found in the ocean 300 miles southwest of Bermuda by search ships and planes had been determined definitely to have come from the two missing KC-135 strato tankers and the debris would be sent to Homestead Air Force Base for study. Apparently both planes crashed together in mid-air, instantly killing all eleven crewmen.

In the preceding story we encountered the procedures of air-sea rescue in full operation. A hunt always begins by working on the assumption that a craft could not break up at sea without leaving many telltale clues such as floating debris, large oil slicks, life saving gear and floating bodies. Some or all will always turn up. If not found at sea, many times they will wash ashore.

When a ditching at sea occurs, emergency signaling equipment such as radios (voice or code), flares and mirrors have been provided as standard equipment on life saving boats and rafts since the early 1940's.

It seems impossible that man and machine could vanish at sea without leaving a clue, but in the "Limbo of the Lost" it happens.

For list of those killed, consult Appendix G.

KB-50 TANKER VANISHES
MONDAY, JANUARY 8, 1962

At approximately one o'clock on the afternoon of Monday, January 8, 1962 the control tower at Langley Air Force Base, Virginia received a radio position report from a KB-50J refueling tanker that took off from the base at 11:17 a.m.

Command pilot Major Tawney reported his plane's position as about 240 miles east of Norfolk, Virginia, estimated time of arrival at Lajes, in the Azores: 6:52 p.m.

When the Air Force tanker failed to contact Langley tower as scheduled at 2:00 p.m., the all too familiar emergency call was made to Coast Guard air-sea rescue headquarters:

"United States Air Force KB-50 tanker plane . . . converted bomber with four piston engines and two jets . . . believed down at sea . . . nine men aboard . . . enough fuel to stay aloft until about midnight."

An air-sea search was concentrated along a path 130 miles wide running east from the missing plane's last reported position. Weather reports in the area - "windy but good, with visibility ten miles."

Among the planes participating in the hunt were thirty-two C-130 turbine-propeller cargo aircraft out of Langley, two Coast Guard Grumman Albatross amphibians based in Bermuda and three Martin Mariner flying boats from Elizabeth City, North Carolina.

Surface vessels in the special search effort included the Coast Guard cutters Escanaba, Campbell and Ingham, plus all merchant ships at sea in the vicinity of the wide spread hunt.

NOTHING FOUND SEARCH CALLED

After five days the Coast Guard headquarters, which co-ordinated the search operations, called the air-sea rescue search off after exhausting every possibility of locating the KB-50 and its crew. According to officials not one single clue was found.

For list of those lost, consult Appendix H.

ARMY, NAVY AND COAST GUARD SEEK C-54
THURSDAY, JULY 3, 1947

Americans everywhere were finalizing plans for Independence Day celebrations, when word was flashed to the Coast Guard, Army Air Corps, and Navy stationed along the lower eastern seaboard, that a four-engined, Army C-54 cargo transport plane with its crew of six was missing at sea. The report stated the overdue aircraft took off Thursday morning, July 3, 1947 from Kindley Field, Bermuda for Morrison Army Air Field, Palm Beach, Florida. Estimated time of arrival was scheduled for mid-afternoon.

Ships and planes raced out to play their role in the by now all to familiar search pattern extending from the coast of Florida to Bermuda. Hunters scanned the seas all night for a glimpse of light. By dawn the air-sea rescue operation was in full swing with hopes high of finding the fliers alive.

WRECKAGE SIGHTED

Early Friday morning, July 4th, a large Army transport C-74 reported sighting wreckage on the sea 300 miles northeast of West Palm Beach, Florida. Army authorities said the Navy cargo ship "Orion" was plowing toward the area in order to determine if the debris was that of the missing plane. The C-74 was acting as guide for the surface craft when poor visibility and communication difficulties hampered and slowed the rescue efforts.

For hours the press awaited word from the "Orion". Finally Major L. R. Humphreys, Commanding the Fifth Air Rescue Squadron at Morrison Field released details of the find. He reported, the cargo ship found an oxygen bottle, two yellow seat cushions and some aircraft plywood all believed to be Army aircraft equipment, but none of it identified as belonging to the lost plane.

SEARCH ENDS - CREW LOST

Air Transport Command (ATC) headquarters announced the search for the C-54 and its crew was officially abandoned as of Tuesday, July 8, 1947. According to the statement, the only wreckage found in the course of the 110,000 square mile search by Army, Navy and Coast Guard planes and surface vessels, was that picked up by the "Orion". No other debris, bodies, oil slick or clues turned up. The ATC alone flew fifty-two sorties involving 422 hours of flight.

All planes and ships in the vicinity of the search route were asked to continue the hunt if at all possible. But to this day the mystery of what happened to the Army C-54 and crew of six remains the secret of the "Limbo of the Lost".

For the names of those lost, consult Appendix I.

HUNT ON FOR LOST
C-133 CARGOMASTER
SUNDAY, SEPTEMBER 22, 1963

It seemed the "Limbo of the Lost" was once again the victor in the sea search for a four-engined Air Force C-133, Cargomaster, lost on a flight between Dover, Delaware and Terceira Island, the Azores.

The plane with ten men on board vanished Sunday, September 22, 1963 after the pilot gave his last position report at 3:00 a.m. as eighty-miles southeast of Cape May, New Jersey.

A twenty-three plane rescue fleet scanned a 640-mile zone, east from the coast between Atlantic City, New Jersey to Virginia Beach, Virginia. Many times search aircraft flew as low as 400 to 600 feet, in parallel east-west tracks covering 80-by-40 miles of ocean, 180 miles southeast of Cape May.

As search planes flew their assigned low level courses, two Coast Guard aircraft circled above at 26,000 feet, coordinating the effort and relaying radio messages between the search planes and their home bases.

OBJECT SIGHTED

On the afternoon of Wednesday, September 25th, Captain James L. Smith of Nahunta, Georgia - pilot of a five-man, twin engined, Grumman amphibian - was ordered from his half searched area to an adjacent sector to his west. Upon arrival at the target he spent several hours circling and dropping smoke markers to guide a Coast Guard cutter to debris. After close examination of the wreckage, it turned out to be of no significance.

*   *   *   *   *   *

A Coast Guard spokesman said search planes sighted pieces of brown and blue metal objects about two feet square, partially submerged, some blue cloth and a three-foot round, light brown object in some six locations, all within a thirty-mile radius about 440 miles east of Cape May, New Jersey. The spokesman said, from the description of the round object, it could have been the fuselage of the missing plane.

Two Coast Guard cutters and three Navy destroyers were sent to the area to examine the wreckage. In the meantime the wide spread hunt was called off pending examination of the find.

The Coast Guard, acting as the search and rescue coordinator, re-ordered the special air-sea search to continue after examination of all the discovered debris proved not to be part of the missing aircraft. They pointed out that hope of finding survivors looked grim.

SEARCH CALLED OFF AS FUTILE

As the day's hunt ended on Wednesday, September 25th, the decision to abandon all hope for the 10 men was made. Many searchers expressed sadness, not wanting to give up, although some said they held little real hope because of high winds and seas that plagued the search area Monday, September 23rd.

Major Robert W. Griswold, a search squadron briefing officer summed up the situation: "The factors that must be weighed included the number of hours a plane is missing, the areas that have been covered and a judgment based on past experience. You've got to stop sometime."

MYSTERY OF THE SARGASSO SEA

Many people believe the answer to the strange disappearances within the "Limbo of the Lost," can be found hidden in the mysterious "Sargasso Sea."

For more than four centuries it has been commonly believed that this area of the Atlantic Ocean was so thick with seaweed that ships could not penetrate it. But tales of floating masses of seaweed capable of stopping the progress of ships is quite fantastic.

LOCATION OF THE SARGASSO SEA

The "Sargasso Sea" lies between the United States and the west coast of Africa. Its eastern boundary is near the Azores, the southern boundary somewhere near the West Indies. The western and northern borders shift considerably from season to season because of changing weather conditions.

Somewhat elliptical in shape, the "Sargasso Sea" can be located between 20° and 35° north latitude (parallels) and 30° and 70° west longitude (meridians).

This unusually quiet region is bound by the clockwise currents of the Gulf stream and North Atlantic current on the west and north; on the south by the equatorial drift and on the east by a line which runs roughly along the submerged mountain ridge in the Middle Atlantic. Because of ocean current variations and the shifting and meandering of the Gulf Stream, the borders of the area are not constant or sharply defined.

Precipitation in the region of the Sargasso Sea is low, evaporation is high, winds are light causing a tropical haze and the water is remarkably clear, warm and extremely salty.

WHAT IS THE SARGASSO SEA?

The noun Sargasso comes from the Portuguese, "Salgazo," derived from a word which stands for tiny grapes. The genus Sargassum, sometimes called Gulfweed, belongs to the brown algae family and bears small but prominent grape-shaped, berry-like bladders. The stems are brown and the finely divided branchlets are covered with slender pointed leaves that vary from olive-yellow to a delicate green.

Sargassum weed is picked up from island and mainland coasts to the southwest by the strong ocean currents, carried away from shore and floats in the mighty Gulf stream until deposited in a huge, quiet pool of seaweed.

Unlike any other part of the oceans of the world this slowly drifting seaweed covers an area about equal in size to that of the entire United States, approximately two-million square miles.

Rather than being continuous, the weeds lie in long

parallel bands of various sizes, some stretching as far as the eye can see. In places the mysterious sea of weeds is very thin, floating only on the surface, while in others it extends far below the surface.

The branchlets of the graceful Sargassum weed shelter hosts of swimming, floating, clinging creatures of strange shapes and habits. Shrimp, crabs, mollusks, and sea spiders with spiny outgrowths colored to imitate the weed, hide among its leaflets. A remarkable nest building fish, the "marbled angler" of brown and yellow coloration, blends exactly with the gulfweed, and weaves gelatinous strings of egg clusters into the plant growth with its spiny hand-like fins. Its nests contains thousands of eggs.

If a branch of the Sargassum weed is shaken, hundreds of many-colored denizens are seen rushing about in all directions, eager to return to the particular spot best adapted to conceal them.

COLUMBUS SAILED THE SARGASSO

On September 16, 1492, six weeks after Christopher Columbus sailed from Cadiz on his first epoch-making voyage, his ships began to notice the unusual plant life of the Sargasso Sea.

He reported in the Journal of his first voyage encountering floating seaweed not far west of the Azores, and by the time he reached mid-ocean there was "such an abundance of weeds that the sea seemed to be covered with them; they came from the west."

Columbus took this for a sure sign that his little fleet of three ships was nearing land, but when they had sailed another week the wind died out and the sea was so calm "that the sailors murmured, saying they had got into smooth water, where it would never blow to carry them back to Spain."

His sailors were naturally terrified for they could not conceive of seaweed without rocks, so to assure them, records show Columbus hove the lead line, and found no bottom. Little did he realize that the ocean bottom lay nearly three miles below.

It was almost a month after Columbus saw the first Sargassum weed before he finally sighted the West Indies on October 14th. He described the weed in great detail in his log, and implied that he had evidence of earlier voyages through the area. He said it was possible the Carthaginians reached the Sargasso as early as 530 B. C.

PHOENICIANS FIRST TELLERS OF TALES

From antiquity down through the Middle Ages, this ocean region was called the "Sea of Darkness." The canny Phoenicians were perhaps the first tellers of the tale, for they frightened off prospective competitors in foreign commerce by dire stories of what awaited any foolhardy voyager beyond the Pillars of Hercules.

The Atlantic, they said, was a place of dreadful darkness, a muddy and a shallow sea, where great morasses of strange growth waited to twine their slimy tendrils about any ship that ventured there and hold it helpless prisoner forever.

The discovery of a large store of Phoenician coins on one of the Azores makes it seem quite certain that those daring navigators from African shores actually saw the Sargasso Sea and embroidered this foundation of fact with their own shrewd fancy.

For centuries later explorers brought back further tales of these strange waters. They believed that all the wrecks and derelicts of the Atlantic eventually drift to the vast pool of weed and there hopelessly tangle in a mat of vegetation, slowly eddy, round and round in desolate assembly until time and shipworms rotted their hulks and sent them to the bottom.

Artists and romancers have exercised their imaginations, even to the fantastic picture of a vast vortex, the later lost ships at the outside, toward the middle old pirate vessels, and in the very center Phoenician galleys still afloat on a voyage which has no end.

Sea lore taught them that the Sargasso Sea was indeed the "Port of Missing Ships," the "Ocean Graveyard" or "Davy Jones's Locker." for under the sluggish weeds were Greek Triremes, Portuguese Caravels and Spanish Galleons.

The medieval mariner peopled the Sargasso with strange monsters and related tales of immense octopi that rose out of its uncanny depths to drag down with their huge tentacles unfortunate vessels entangled in the weed.

In olden times sailors believed that the entire Sargasso

was filled with weeds and that a ship might be lost forever by being caught in gigantic seaweed growths; and of crews becoming paralyzed by the breathless air, until they died of suffocation or hunger.

Until disillusioning scholars plumbed all the depths of the "Sea of Darkness," scores of unsolved mysteries of the sea had been attributed to the Sargasso.

THE "LOST" CONTINENT OF ATLANTIS

Dreamers imagined that somewhere among the seaweed of the Sargasso Sea was to be found the lost continent of Atlantis.

Atlantis was the creation of old and inaccurate chroniclers who gathered and warped miscellaneous data of history and physical phenomena. All the stories of the powerful capital as outlined by the Greek Philosopher Plato are now known to be pure fabrication, fiction and folklore.

It was told that Atlantis was a huge island in the sea west of Gibraltar. This dream country, the thread of whose legend may be traced through the folklore and priestcraft of a dozen countries, was thought to occupy most of the space where the Atlantic now lies. Thousands of years ago, the armies of this rich and powerful, happy land had dominated much of North Africa and Western Europe, but the Greeks had halted their march of conquest.

Suddenly an upheaval of nature overwhelmed the country by an onrushing sea causing the entire island-continent to sink beneath the waves. This is supposed to be the origin of the Flood story, which is so curiously and inexplicably universal.

Ancient accounts of this island have stimulated men's imaginations for centuries, inspiring extensive scientific research of the Sargasso Sea in modern times.

SUMMATION

Now that both poles have been conquered, and men have scaled Mt. Everest, and Africa and Australia have ceased to be unknown continents, scientists are planning explorations to the very floor of the seas.

Man has eliminated the mermaid and merman, but has confirmed the wildest imaginations of sea serpents in the existence of the giant octopus. He has discovered stranger deep-sea fishes than even a drug stimulated hallucination could conceive.

We know now that no ship need fear permanent entanglement in the Sargasso Sea, and that in this "Port of Missing Ships" man can expect to find nothing more than a few bits of debris, such as might be seen on any other part of the ocean. It is merely a comparatively quiet spot, the hub of a huge, vaguely defined circle of seaweed, the spawning ground of the common eel.

Far from being the region of dread pictured by medieval mariners, the Sargasso Sea is to men of natural history, oceanography, botany and geology a paradise of strange and fascinating rewards.

It is indeed a wonderful area, and we must marvel at

the courage of Columbus, who led his crews across this mysterious trackless, seemingly treacherous area.

Professional seamen who regularly cruise to Bermuda, which lies in the middle of this sea of weeds, must smile when a green frightened seaman asks about the weird stories of the Sargasso Sea.

CHAPTER IV

STEAMSHIPS THAT BECAME FAMOUS THROUGH TRAGEDY

MARINE SULPHUR QUEEN OVERDUE
THURSDAY, FEBRUARY 7, 1963

The "SS Marine Sulphur Queen", a T2-SE-A1 type tank vessel, under the Command of Captain James V. Fanning, steamed out of Beaumont, Texas on the afternoon of Saturday, February 2, 1963. Her cargo was 15,260 tons of hot, molten sulphur-brimstone to be delivered to Norfolk, Virginia by the afternoon of February 7th.

At 1:25 a.m. (EST), about 35 hours after departing Beaumont, the bulk carrier reported its position near Dry Tortugas in the Gulf, 200 miles off Key West, in the straits of Florida. She was operating normally and on schedule. At that time a seaman dispatched a personal radio message regarding some stock purchases. An attempt to send a reply to him went undelivered as contact could not be made with the "Sulphur Queen".

LONG OVERDUE

When the big tanker didn't report as scheduled at Norfolk, authorities became concerned and tried to establish radio contact with her. No answer.

The situation was reported to air-sea rescue headquarters and a search was launched. Coast Guard vessels and aircraft were dispatched from Virginia, North Carolina, Florida and Louisiana.

Miami's U. S. Weather Bureau reported that the tanker's course would have taken her through the "Limbo of the Lost" area during a severe Atlantic storm that battered the southeastern coast of the United States with winds of thirty-five knots.

DEBRIS DISCOVERED

A Navy patrol plane reported sighting debris 200 miles east of Jacksonville, Florida. Coast Guard officials at Jacksonville Beach said the pilot radioed that the debris consisted of "sticks of wood, several big white objects and a large amount of yellow substance."

The missing tanker had a white superstructure, but the spokesman would not speculate whether the wreckage might be that of the tanker until an on the spot confirmation was made.

Coast Guard patrol boat "Sweet Gum", was the first to arrive at the scene. Upon close examination she radioed that the reported debris was definitely not from the "Marine Sulphur Queen".

SEARCH EXTENDED

It was eight days since any word had been received from the "Queen" and no clues existed, compounding the mystery. The area covered was expanded from Texas to Virginia. Planes and ships ranged as far out as 280 miles into the Atlantic.

Clearing skies over the search area brought out virtually all Coast Guard aircraft stationed along the Atlantic and Gulf coasts. Merchant ships following or crossing the tanker's intended route were asked to report any sign of debris.

SEARCH ABANDONED

After eight days of scouring the sea not so much as a sliver of wood belonging to the "Sulphur Queen" had been found. Without any clues and the possibility negative of finding the crew alive, Coast Guard officials abandoned the search.

Board Chairman and President of the Marine Transport Corporation, Mr. H. L. White, sent official condolences to the wife of the "Sulphur Queen's" Captain indicating the company had given up hope of finding the 39-member crew of the missing ship alive. The telegram received by Mrs. Fanning said the company regretted to inform her that the Coast Guard had given up its search as of February 15, 1963.

Three days later, five widows of the licensed Officers of the lost bulk carrier filed suit in Federal Court asking $2,500,000 damages from the ships owners.

DEBRIS OF SULPHUR QUEEN FOUND

On February 20, 1963, a Navy torpedo retriever boat found a life jacket marked "Sulphur Queen" 14 miles southeast of Key West, Florida. Another Coast Guard patrol vessel sent to the area found a second marked life jacket. Immediately an intensive area wide search was again launched by surface craft and airplanes in hope of finding possible survivors.

Before the new hunt was called off, seven life preservers, one apparently used, four life rings, with a man's shirt attached to one, some pieces of the ship's name board and miscellaneous debris were found and brought ashore. A tentative Coast Guard evaluation of the evidence was that perhaps two crew members survived and then drowned, or were attacked by sharks or barracuda.

SULPHUR QUEEN HEARING CONVENED

On Monday, March 24, 1963, a United States Coast Guard Board of Investigation was convened.

Day after day in the hearing rooms Coast Guard Officers searched for clues to the mystery of the "Marine Sulphur Queen's" disappearance. Inquiries were made as to the ships construction, the properties and behavior of molten sulphur and the careful retracing of the ships full history. Officials of the Marine Transport Lines, which owned her, and the men who helped rebuild the old T-2 tanker into a special carrier, took the stand and added their bits of information, agreeing to the completeness of the mystery, filling in small pieces.

THEORIES ABOUND

Hijacked or captured:

Maybe the tanker was hijacked or she just simply drifted into Cuban waters and was seized.

If either had happened word would have been received by the time the air-sea search was called off. This theory was abandoned.

Exploded, hit stray mine or sabotaged:

Maybe the bulk carrier had exploded, leaking sulphur gas exploded, or possibly she hit a stray mine or was sabotaged.

According to officials of the missing tanker's owner, "Marine Transport Lines of New York", sulphur, kept in a liquid state, with 265 degree steel coils, was as safe as most cargoes. Regarding sabotage or hitting a mine, the possibility was so remote that it was dismissed.

A Coast Guard officer said, that if sulphur should come in contact with sea water, the ship "would go up like an atom bomb." Expert witnesses including a chemist associated with the Texas Sulphur Company, shipper of the cargo, testified that scientists did not believe that molten sulphur could explode, even if sea water entered the tanks.

Broke in half:

Maybe because of the storm she broke in half or was

capsized by a great wave.

Seamen familiar with the missing tanker testified that ships like the "Queen" just didn't go down very fast, at least so fast that she wouldn't be able to get off an emergency radio message. If she was being battered badly enough to break up, or the seas so rough she could be capsized, the Captain surely would have sent out a distress signal. The "Queen" carried two high frequency radio transmitters with emergency batteries and she also had a radio telephone.

Several ships of the "Marine Sulphur Queen's" class had cracked and split. But no evidence was developed to explain how this ship, even if she had split in half could go down so quickly as to leave no trace.

Hundreds of the T-2 type tankers were built on a World War II design and did valiant service in the war. In the nature of such production-line ship construction there were bugs. Quite a few broke in two, ten to be exact, but in all cases the halves or at least one half remained afloat. Most of the pieces were salvaged.

Officials of the ship line announced that another sulphur-ship was on order, a converted ship that would use the stern of a T-2 that had been cut in two.

Witnesses told of a series of minor fires which surrounded the special tanks carrying the hot sulphur. They said these fires appeared to be from gases, and one likened them to burning cognac around Christmas pudding, in that they flared up and then were quickly spent.

An expert on explosives for the Department of the

Interior's Bureau of Mines testified that gases formed by impurities in sulphur might have exploded. However, such an explosion probably would have been moderate because of escape vents.

SULPHUR QUEEN HEARING YIELDS LITTLE

All evidence presented only added to the mystery. Even though some items were discovered, the question of what happened to the thirty-nine bodies of the crew still remained. Why were no lifeboats, oil slick or floating sulphur found? Why was no distress message sent?

On Monday, May 27, 1963 the special "Coast Guard Board of Inquiry" headed by Rear Admiral James D. Craik ended. The report read, "No final conclusions as to the exact cause of the disappearance of the tanker could be offered." The "SS Marine Sulphur Queen" and her entire crew must be presumed lost. (See Appendix J for names of lost). The Admiral called the inquiry one of the longest in recent years, but without the satisfaction of reaching a concrete conclusion.

With those words, the "Marine Sulphur Queen" was written off as just one more unsolved mystery in the "Limbo of the Lost".

LLOYD'S REGISTER OF SHIPPING

71, Fenchurch Street, London, E.C.3

Telegraphic \ Inland: Committee, London, Telex
Address ∫ Overseas: Committee, London, E.C.3

Telephone: 01-709 9166
Telex No.: 24305

Air Mail

Your Ref: JWS/tkw   2nd May 1969

*Please address further
communications on this subject
to THE SECRETARY
and quote the following
reference*

Statistics

Dear Sir,

       With reference to previous correspondence,
and your letter of the 22nd April in particular, I have
made a "dummy run" investigating within the perameters
of your enquiry from both ends of the time span. The
basis of our interpretation of your requirements is the
category of loss we call "Missing". During the period
1962 to 1967 inclusive, only one ship, the former T-2
tanker the "MARINE SULPHUR QUEEN", flying the
American flag of 7,240 tons gross was posted as missing in
in this area. She had been converted to a molten sulphur
carrier, with which she was loaded at the time, and was
on her way from Beaumont to Norfolk, Virginia, when she
disappeared in approximately latitude 26' 40° North
longtitude 88' 0° West on the 3rd February 1963. I
remember this case well because of the dangerous
constituency of the cargo and volatile gas given off
(Hydrogen Sulphide). Doubtless you can find more from
the government enquiry which was made into this case
for there was considerable loss of life.

       I investigated the years 1890 to 1893 inclusive
and discovered forty seven cases of ships missing.

TREASURY DEPARTMENT
UNITED STATES COAST GUARD

ADDRESS REPLY TO:
COMMANDANT
U.S. COAST GUARD
HEADQUARTERS
WASHINGTON 25, D.C.

AUG 23 1963

From: Marine Board of Investigation
To: Commandant (MVI)

Subj: SS MARINE SULPHUR QUEEN; disappearance of at sea on or about
       4 February 1963

1. At about 1830, CST, 2 February 1963, the SS MARINE SULPHUR QUEEN, with
a crew of 39 and a full cargo of approximately 15,260 long tons of molten
sulphur, took departure from Sabine Sea Buoy on a voyage from Beaumont,
Texas to Norfolk, Virginia and subsequently disappeared at sea without the
transmission of a radio distress message.

2. The SS MARINE SULPHUR QUEEN, O.N. 245295 (Ex-ESSO NEW HAVEN) was an
all-welded T2-SE-A1, tankship; of 7240 gross tons and 4057 net tons;
length 504 ft., breadth 68.2 ft., and depth 39.2 ft.; built at Sun
Shipbuilding and Drydock Co., Chester, Pa. in 1944 and converted to a
molten sulphur carrier at Bethlehem Steel Co. Shipyard, Baltimore, Md.,
during the latter part of 1960. The vessel was single screw, powered
by a 7240 shaft horsepower turbo-electric drive manufactured by Westing-
house Elec. & Mfg. Co. The vessel was owned by Marine Sulphur Transport
Corporation and operated under a bareboat charter by Marine Transport
Lines, Inc., both companies being located at 11 Broadway, New York, N.Y.
The conversion to a molten sulphur carrier was accomplished in accordance
with plans approved by the U. S. Coast Guard and the American Bureau of
Shipping.

3. The vessel was certificated by the U. S. Coast Guard at Baltimore,
Md. on 18 January 1961 for the carriage of "Grade E liquids at elevated
temperatures" and classed by the American Bureau of Shipping as to hull
and machinery. The vessel was recertificated by the U. S. Coast Guard
at Beaumont, Texas on 17 January 1963 and retained in class by the
American Bureau of Shipping at the same time. The vessel had valid load
line certificates, both International and Coastwise, issued by the
American Bureau of Shipping and valid radio certificates issued by the
Beaumont, Texas office of the Federal Communications Commission covering
both the installed radio equipment and the lifeboat portable radio.

82

NAVY COLLIER CYCLOPS MISSING
MARCH 13, 1918

The big 14,500 ton American Naval fuel supply ship, "U. S. S. Cyclops" was reported overdue at her Atlantic port of destination, Norfolk, Virginia. Navy Department officials said the 540 foot collier, built in 1910 and considered the last word in marine construction, steamed from Bahia, Brazil on January 28, 1918 with a cargo of manganese, much needed by the allied nations at war with Germany.

First stop scheduled on the long voyage was Georgetown, in the British West Indies on March 3rd, to take on coal. The following day she headed out to sea bound for Norfolk but with one of her two engines damaged. Naval authorities quickly pointed out, the "Cyclops" had enough power to be driven at ten-knots an hour even with one engine. In any event the engine problem would not have prevented the collier from communicating by radio. If her main engines were totally disabled the big ship would still be capable of using her radio plant.

The only civilian listed among the passengers was the United States Consul-General at Rio de Janeiro. Other passengers were two U. S. Marine Lieutenants, seventy Naval Enlisted Men returning to the United States, plus the ship's crew of fifteen Naval Reserve Officers and 221 Enlisted Personnel.

At the peak of World War I, on January 8, 1918, the "Cyclops" had been detached from her Atlantic fleet group at Virginia and assigned to the Overseas Transport Service with the U. S. Navy.

SEARCH FOR CYLCOPS UNDERWAY

When the big supply ship was reported as missing, Secretary of the Navy Daniels ordered an unremitting search of trade routes by American and French Naval and Merchant vessels. He ordered that every quarter, every rod of the "Cyclops' " route be covered; every one of the scores of islands and isolated bays be entered and every beach which dots that portion of the sea be scrutinized.

At a press conference Mr. Daniels' Chief Assistant reported, "Hope is still felt by the Navy. We refuse to give up the search until every possibility of finding some trace of the collier has been exhausted."

NO TRACE - NAVY MYSTIFIED

Although a thorough search was conducted of the probable course the big ship would have followed, not a trace or information concerning her had been obtained. Radio calls from every possible point were beamed to the "Cyclops", but to no avail. Every day of the search only resulted in the deepening of the mystery.

On April 16th, a spokesman from the Office of the Secretary of the Navy reported, "No well-founded reason can be given to explain the "Cyclops" being overdue. We refuse to believe that the collier could have been wiped out without leaving a trace."

For the first time since the hunt began the Navy officially went on record as saying, "The search still continues, but the Navy feels extremely anxious as to the safety of the "Cyclops" and her 309 passengers and crew."

WHAT HAPPENED TO THE CYCLOPS?

Explanations for the collier's disappearance were offered from every quarter.

Sub-raider or floating mine:

There were many advocates of the theory that the "Cyclops" struck a floating mine, or a German U-Boat was responsible for her disappearance.

A Navy Department statement read, "There have been no reports that would indicate the presence of either submarines or mines in the locality of the "Cyclops" route. Further, certainly debris or lifeboats would have been found." After the war German Admiralty records revealed, no submarines were in the waters of the West Indies during March and April of 1918.

Hurricane or severe storm:

It was admitted that the possibility of a sudden hurricane, not infrequent in those waters, might have first disabled and then engulfed the "Cyclops".

According to official records there were no reports of a hurricane or stormy weather conditions in the area in which the collier would have had to pass. Even if such a disaster did occur, why wasn't any debris found?

Hijacking:

The conjecture that enemy agents might have gained control in a midnight mutiny was imposed.

Naval officials said that even in such a well nigh impossible event, lack of coal would have prevented an attempt to start on a long transatlantic voyage. Further, German Admiralty records captured after the war did not indicate the occurrence of such a plot.

Explosion:

Another theory offered was that an internal explosion such as a time bomb might have destroyed the vessel's wireless and motive power at one instant, or the manganese ore, with which the collier was heavily laden, might, under certain conditions, give off an extremely dangerous gas that exploded.

The Navy Department reported that precautions had been taken against this on all ships engaged in the manganese carrying trade. If either had happened, the ship itself or surface wreckage would remain to mark her grave.

Traitor:

The most vicious explanation offered was that of "traitor". That the "Cyclops' " Captain met, by pre-arrangement, a German U-Boat and assisted in over-powering the other Americans aboard. This circum-stantial accusation was built upon the fact that Lieutenant-Commander, George W. Worley, of the United States Reserve Force, and Captain of the "Cyclops", was German born. Also before he sailed on this last voyage he disposed of some property he owned in Norfolk, Virginia, including the home his wife and daughter lived in. He told friends that when he returned from the voyage he intended to get an extended leave of absence and go back to California and rest. He said he had to have an operation performed and it would take about six months for him to recover his strength.

Worley came to the United States as a child, from Germany and was adopted by a man in California. When Worley grew up he applied to the courts to change his name from George Frederick Wichman to that of the man who had befriended him. In 1893 he became an American citizen.

When this traitor theory was told to Mrs. Worley by reporters she became very angry. She said her husband was a good American and that his long and faithful record in the government service proved it.

She refused to believe her husband dead, instead she believed the "Cyclops" was probably disabled at sea and that her husband was waiting to be picked up.

In answer to questions about her husband, Mrs.

Worley replied, "Do you think my husband would prove a traitor to America, to his wife and little daughter? My husband was and is an American through and through. He hated Germany. He came here seeking freedom and he would fight and die to maintain that freedom. He is just as good an American as any man born in America, and a whole lot better than many of those who question his patriotism now. I hope my husband is alive to settle with his accusers."

The traitor theory was eliminated once and for all when after the war it was not supported by captured German Admiralty records.

CYCLOPS DISAPPEARANCE BAFFLING

The "U. S. S. Cyclops" was modern, staunch, well manned and equipped. To those who are familiar with the sea and navigation, the disappearance of the big collier is inexplicable.

Wreckage of other ships had floated ashore to tell their fate, but no such messenger with a vestige of debris ever arrived to tell the tale of the mysterious disappearance of the "Cyclops".

The facts surrounding the big ship were released on Thursday, April 11, 1918, almost a month after being reported overdue at Norfolk. The U. S. Naval censor requested that the wire press services not publish the information on the grounds that the "Cyclops" had not been given up as lost and to publish the fact that she was overdue might expose her to submarine or other enemy attack while possibly disabled on the high seas.

The "Cyclops" was finally given up as lost without explanation after a month and a half of futile searching and her name officially stricken from the Naval Register.

ANOTHER ANSWER TO THE FATE OF CYCLOPS

Almost eight year later on December 3, 1925, interest in the "Cyclops" was revived in official circles when Secretary Wilbur received from the commandant of the Fifth Naval District a report that the "Orion", also a Naval collier, had been placed in drydock with hull amidships buckled and twisted, and her forepeak tanks flooded.

The day before on December 2nd, the "Orion", loaded with a cargo of coal, sailed out of Hampton Roads bound for Melville, Rhode Island. Later that same afternoon, just outside the Virginia Capes, she encountered stormy weather and was forced to return to port.

As the "Orion" was a sister ship of the "Cyclops", identical in size and construction, Secretary of the Navy Wilbur ordered a careful inspection and inquiry into the exact cause of the buckling and other damage. He believed whatever caused the trouble could possibly have been linked to the mysterious disappearance of the "Cyclops". It did not!

At this point we must place the name of the "U. S. S. Cyclops" on the list of those in the "Port of Missing Ships" in the "Limbo of the Lost".

FREIGHTER SUDUFFCO VANISHED
MARCH 13, 1926

The Freighter "Suduffco", under the Command of a Captain T. Turner, sailed from Port Newark, New Jersey for Los Angeles, California on March 13, 1926 with a crew of twenty-eight. In her hold was a mixed cargo of 4,000 tons, including a large shipment of steel pipe valued at $500,000. She was scheduled to have gone through the Panama Canal on March 22nd but never arrived.

On April 7th, the Transmarine Corporation of Port Newark, fearing for the safety of the ship and her crew, requested that the Navy Department initiate a search for their missing freighter. Also they ordered two of the "Suduffco's" sister ships into the search - the "Suboatco" took the Gulf of Mexico and the "Sucaresco" hunted along the west coast.

An official of the Transmarine Corporation added, because of the experience of her master, they felt sure the "Suduffco" would be found. Captain Turner commanded ships of the American Line for twenty-five years and during the War was in charge of an American Transport. He was known as a man who could handle a ship in any situation.

ABANDON HOPE FOR SHIP AND CREW

After more than two weeks of searching by the Army, Navy and Coast Guard in the Atlantic, Gulf of Mexico and along the west coast, the Transmarine Corporation announced that as of April 27th the quest had been given up. A Company official stated, it was as though the "Suduffco" had been swallowed by some sort of gigantic sea monster.

Whatever happened to the "Suduffco" and her crew will never be known. Nothing has ever been found, therefore we are left no other choice than to place her name on the ghostly honor roll along with those of other ships that have sailed into "The Limbo of the Lost".

CHAPTER V

THREE DERELICTS,
A TRAINING SHIP AND A TALE

CLASSIC STORY OF MARY CELESTE
WEDNESDAY, DECEMBER 4, 1872

On the afternoon of Wednesday, December 4, 1872, the "Dei Gratia", ("By Grace of God"), a British brigantine, out of New York since November 15th, was sailing between the Azores and Portugal, heading for Gibraltar. At one o'clock the ship's Captain, David R. Morehouse sighted a vessel, also a brigantine, "Mary Celeste", seemingly in trouble about four or five miles off. Her sails were torn, she was listing badly, no sailors were on deck nor anyone at her wheel, yet she was not displaying a distress signal.

Captain Morehouse ordered three men to board her and render assistance if needed. About one hour later the bewildered sailors reported that no one was aboard, alive or dead. It was as though the entire ship's company of ten, including the ship's cat vanished into thin air.

There were no boats on board, all hatch doors were wide open, the wheel was operating freely and the compass stand was knocked out of place and the compass broken. Chronometer, Sextant, Ship's register and navigation book were nowhere to be found. However, the ships log, showing regular daily entries, was located in the mate's cabin. The working log, a slate kept by the mate, showed that at 8 o'clock on the morning of Monday, November 25th, the "Mary Celeste" passed six miles off the eastern tip of Saint Mary's Island, (Santa Marie, the Azores), about 800 miles from Portugal.

Her cargo of 1,701 barrels of alcohol, worth about 42 thousand dollars, was intact in the hold covered by three to four feet of sea water. The galley was in perfect order and the dinner table was clean, indicating that the crew was not about to eat. No wine, beer or spirits were allowed on board as Captain Benjamin Spooner Briggs was a firm believer in temperance.

In the crew's quarters, the seamen's personal belongings were untouched. Their lockers contained various items of value, including money and the one thing no mariner would ever leave behind, his pipe. In the Captain's cabin the berth was unmade and on the floor were his boots and raincoat.

All the evidence pointed to one conclusion, the vessel had been abandoned hastily, sometime between 8:00 a.m. and noon.

As Captain Morehouse studied the situation I am sure he could not help but think back to the evening of November 5th, two days before the "Mary Celeste" set sail for Genoa. He probably recalled having had dinner with the 37-year-old Captain, Ben Briggs and his wife Sarah in New York. It was the custom in those days that the wife and children of the ship's master accompanied him to sea.

MARY CELESTE SALVAGED

Captain Morehouse discussed the matter of the "Mary Celeste" with his first mate who wanted to claim the derelict for the salvage money. After a lengthy discussion the Captain agreed, but explained that they had 600 miles to go before reaching the nearest port of Gibraltar, and he could only spare two seamen besides the mate as a crew. Knowing fully the dangers involved, they set off sailing side by side.

Luckily the weather remained calm for six days. Then on December 11th, as they sighted Cape Spartel, Morocco, a vicious storm of high winds and pelting rain began. During the night the two ships lost sight of one another.

On December 12th the "Dei Gratia" reached Gibraltar and the next day the "Mary Celeste" arrived. The mate, with his crew of two, certainly earned consideration for a generous salvage reward, the hard way. But the battle for the spoils was just beginning.

A salvage hearing began on December 18th and lasted until March 14, 1873. Captain Morehouse and his crew were accused of foul play, conspiracy and murder. When all was said and done the owners and crew of the "Dei Gratia" were cleared and divided $8,300, certainly a poor reward for their deed.

MARY CELESTE JINX SHIP

The story really began ten years earlier in 1861. The "Mary Celeste", then named "Amazon", was launched at Spencer Island shipyard, Nova Scotia. She was registered in a nearby port on June 10th. The first Captain was a Robert McLellan who died of pneumonia nine days after the ship's registration.

The second skipper was Captain John (Jack) Nutting Parker. He took over and sailed to Portland, Maine. On the return voyage the "Amazon" crashed into a fishing boat. Both craft were extensively damaged.

After repairs the jinx ship set sail for London, then to France, but in the straits of Dover she ran into a brig, sending it to the bottom.

On November 9, 1867, the "Amazon" ran ashore at Cow Bay, Cape Breton Island. The situation appeared hopeless, so she was abandoned to salvage. To make matters worse the "Amazon" was not covered by insurance, and was sold for a small sum, just as she lay.

Alexander McBean purchased the craft, pulled it off the shore and placed her back in service. Twelve months later in November 1868, without an explanation, McBean sold the "Amazon" at auction in New York.

The new owner changed her registry from British to American and also changed her name to "Mary Celeste". She sailed the seas for about a year, but the new owner had no luck with her. Subsequently she was seized in New York and sold for the debt.

From 1866 to 1872 a variety of minor catastrophes befell the owners and captains of the "Mary Celeste". This takes us back to the beginning of the story, but it doesn't end here.

END OF MARY CELESTE

For twelve years after her abandonment in 1872, the "Mary Celeste" sailed the oceans. In December 1884, Captain Gilman C. Parker of Winthrop, Massachusetts, took her to sea from Boston and deliberately smashed the brigantine into a coral reef near Haiti in the West Indies for insurance money.

The plot was discovered and Captain Parker was tried, but on a legal technicality was found innocent and released. Captain Parker didn't win, for he was never allowed to sail as a sea Captain again. In July, 1891 he died, a broken man.

"Mary Celeste" will always rank as the number one derelict, jinx ship that voyaged into the unknown seas of the "Limbo of the Lost".

WHAT HAPPENED TO THE
CREWS OF COLITE AND RUBICON?

Gloria Colite, February 3, 1940:

The 125 foot Schooner "Gloria Colite" of St. Vincent, British West Indies, was sighted on the afternoon of Febuary 3, 1940, apparently abandoned. Her reported position was about 150 miles south of Mobile, Alabama.

The U. S. Coast Guard Cutter "Cardigan", which was operating in the Gulf was sent to the scene. She took the derelict in tow and the cutter's Captain radioed that the vessel's decks were a mass of wreckage, her deck housing smashed and her foresails were set, but badly torn. Her mainsail, rigging and steering were gone and no trace of her crew was found. No clues were uncovered that could shed any light as to why her crew left the schooner at the mercy of the sea.

On the afternoon of February 5th, the "Cardigan" arrived at Mobile with her charge. A full investigation was launched, but without success.

Rubicon, October 22, 1944:

Another noted maritime abandonment mystery occurred on October 22, 1944. This time a Cuban cargo ship, the "Rubicon", of approximately ninety gross tons was found adrift and apparently abandoned in the Gulf stream thirty miles southeast of Key Largo, Florida.

A Navy blimp spotted the ship and notified the Coast Guard at Miami. Two boats were dispatched to investigate, but when they arrived at the scene they found the derelict ship "Rubicon" had already been taken in tow under salvage law by the "Nirvana", a banana boat of United States Registry.

Eighteen hours later all four vessels put into the quarantine dock at Miami and a full investigation was begun. It was noted that the only living creature on board the "Rubicon" was a half starved dog. The lifeboats were gone and a broken hawser was hanging over the bow; otherwise she was apparently in excellent shape. The last entry in the ship's log was dated September 26th, when she apparently put into Havana Harbor. This information only added to the mystery because the air distance from Havana to the spot where she was picked up is estimated at some two hundred miles. There seems to be no logical explanation for the obvious abandonment.

DERELICTS STILL A MYSTERY

To this day, nobody, anywhere has been able to say for sure what became of the crews of the "Gloria Colite" or the "Rubicon". It appears they became just another unfortunate part of the maritime mystery surrounding the "Limbo of the Lost".

ATALANTA FEARED LOST

In January, 1880, Captain Francis Stirling, Master of the British training ship "Atalanta", set sail for the long voyage back to England from the sunny shores of Bermuda. He planned to arrive at Spithead about March 1st with his charge of over 300 young seamen trainees.

When the "Atalanta" was reported as two weeks overdue the British Channel Squadron and the dispatch vessel "Salamis" left Gibraltar in search of her.

A dispatch from Portsmouth, England on April 26th read "No news had been received in reference to the 'Atalanta'." Even the most optimistic were beginning to lose heart.

One of the many search ships returned to England in May with the sad news that there was nothing to report and most likely all those aboard the training ship were lost at sea forever.

The only hope now remaining was a desperate supposition that the "Atalanta" may have been driven far to the north. British Admiralty officials said they received 150 telegrams and 200 personal requests that the coasts of Greenland and Iceland be thoroughly searched.

CONFLICTING REPORTS RECEIVED

First report came from the British Gunboat "Avon" which sighted masses of wreckage from an unidentified vessel off the Azores, close to the usual route of training ships.

Nothing was discovered in the waters bearing the training ship's name and after a further search of the area proved fruitless, Admiral Hood's British channel squadron headed to Bantry Bay. He expected to arrive on or about May 8th for further orders.

* * * * * *

In April 1880, a report was circulated that the steamer "Tamar", from the West Indies, passed a capsized, copper bottomed ship.

Conjecture associated this report with the "Atalanta", but the good Captain of the "Tamar" contradicted the whole story saying he saw no such vessel.

* * * * * *

On April 28th the British Admiralty received word that a bottle had been picked up at the junction of the Weaver and Mersey rivers containing a paper inscribed, "H.M.S. Atalanta, 16th March - fearful hurricane; dismasted; going down fast."

After an investigation a statement was released saying, the message was undoubtedly a discreditable hoax.

* * * * * *

On April 20th, Her Majesty's store ship "Wye" left Gibraltar to search the area of Vigo Bay, Spain, where portions of a wrecked vessel washed ashore.

She arrived at Plymouth, England on April 29th and reported that nothing new had been discovered relating to the fate of the missing training ship.

* * * * * *

On June 2nd, the Captain of a vessel which arrived at Queenstown from Demerara reported that on April 30th, in latitude $30°$ north, longitude $60°$ west, he passed a raft. It was apparently made on board a man-of-war or a first class steamer, because it was bolted together, not lashed. Two days later he said he saw several corpses dressed in white. Rumor had it that another vessel saw the same raft and two corpses dressed as Naval seamen.

Speculation was that the rafts and the missing training ship were related, but it was never proved.

* * * * * *

On June 15th, a special dispatch from Rockport, Massachusetts read, "Captain Edward Millett picked up a bottle floating in the water about a mile off Boston Harbor, containing a leaf from a pocket memorandum-book, on which was written, with great apparent haste, the following: 'April 17, 1880: Training ship Atalanta. We are sinking in longitude $27°$, latitude $32°$, any person finding this note will please advertise in the daily paper, John L. Hutchings, distress'."

* * * * * *

On June 21st, some children playing on the beach at Cow Bay, Nova Scotia, picked up a piece of barrel stave on which the following was written with a lead pencil: "Atalanta going down, April 12, 1880; no hope; send this to Mrs. Mary White, Piers, Sussex. James White."

The piece of wood appeared to have been in the water about two months. The place where it was picked up is about twelve miles east of Halifax and opens directly into the Atlantic Ocean.

* * * * * *

On August 7th, the Admiralty office received a telegram from St. John, New Brunswick, reporting the finding of the "Atalanta's" figurehead. The dispatch was described as being of the sensational type, saying that the vessel had been in collision with an iceberg.

Investigation revealed that no figurehead had been found and that no such vessel entered the port at St. John. The whole story was therefore listed as a fabrication.

REPORT OF INVESTIGATION COMMITTEE

The report of the Investigating Committee on the loss of the British training ship "Atalanta", was published on December 29, 1880, and stated no reliable trace had been found. The committee said they considered the "Atalanta" a very stable ship, except at the large angles of the heel, and that the alterations in her rig only tended to increase her safety. The committee spoke favorably of her officers and crew and pointed out that at the time of her loss, exceptional storms proved fatal to a number of merchant vessels. The only exception was that survivors or debris in the other cases were always found.

Experts agreed that the "Atalanta" must have encountered stormy weather, but so did scores of other vessels that crossed the Atlantic Ocean at the same time, yet the other vessels met with no mishaps other than slight delays. They pointed out that a British Naval vessel was much safer than a merchant ship.

If military men could not manage a well equipped sailing vessel in a storm, what would happen to them if they found themselves in mid ocean on board a disabled ironclad?

The only sure fact is that the staunch and well-fitted "Atalanta" sailed into the port of the "Limbo of the Lost" and was never afterward heard from.

MYTH OF THE FLYING DUTCHMAN

While talking to groups about the mystery of the "Limbo of the Lost", invariably someone asks about the "Flying Dutchman", therefore I have included this section.

As far as I can determine, the legend began in the mid 1600's. Superstitious seamen told tales about a Captain Vanderdecken from Holland who, during a violent storm, was trying to round the Cape of Good Hope. The crew and passengers, fearing for their lives, requested that Captain Vanderdecken turn back, for it was certain that everyone aboard would surely be lost at sea. The phantom sea captain, puffing on his huge pipe, laughed at their request and at the top of his voice began singing irreverent songs. As he cursed, his masts snapped under the force of the winds and his sails carried away. The people again begged him for their lives, but to no avail.

When his first mate tried to force him to take the ship to shelter in a nearby bay, the mad captain flung him overboard. Upon seeing this the crew and passengers began to pray for help. As if in answer to their prayers, an angel or maybe even God himself appeared before the Captain.

With many variations, the conversation was said to go something like this:

Vision . . . "You are very stubborn."

Captain . . . "And you're a rascal . . . I do not want a peaceful voyage . . . I will round the Cape if it takes me to Judgement Day . . . I ask nothing of you, so get clear before I blow out your brains."

When the Vision did not move, Captain Vanderdecken picked up his pistol and fired. Bewildered, because the bullet did not seem to interfere with the Vision, he tried to strike it with his fist, but his arm became paralyzed. He cursed and blasphemed and called God a variety of impious names.

Vision . . . "From this time on you are accursed, condemned to sail upon the high seas without rest or anchorage or port of any kind. You shall have neither beer nor tobacco and vinegar shall be your drink and red-hot coal your meat. It will always be your watch and you will not be able to sleep, for when you close your eyes, a sword shall pierce your body. Since it has been your sport to torment sailors, torment them you will. You will be known as the evil spirit of the sea. You will cross all latitudes of the southern seas without relief or rest and misfortune will befall all who cross your bow. On Judgment Day you will be claimed by the devil."

Captain Vanderdecken's answer to all that was simply, "A fig for the devil." With that last comment the "Vision", crew and passengers vanished. Damned and alone except for his demon cabin-boy, he sailed the seas plaguing mariners.

* * * * * *

Legend has it that whenever the "Flying Dutchman" was seen, catastrophe occurred, such as:

A false course set, then shipwreck.

Wine turned sour and all food became beans.

Sometimes the "Flying Dutchman" would send letters to the Captain of a ship meeting her, if read, the ship was lost.

If a boat was sent alongside the Phantom ship, it would disappear with all hands.

* * * * * *

The "Flying Dutchman" would on occasion change the appearance of his ship so that it was not readily recognized. It was said that the "Flying Dutchman" gathered a collection of seamen as cursed as himself; all criminals, pirates and cowards.

For the mariner of those days and even until the late 1800's, the story was told and believed by many. I am the first to admit that anything is possible at sea, but I must also add, it is highly unlikely that there ever was a "Flying Dutchman".

CHAPTER VI

PIRACY ON THE HIGH SEAS

STRANGE CASE OF CAROL DEERING

One of the strangest mysteries of the "Limbo of the Lost" involved the five-masted, 3,500 ton, American schooner, "Carol (Carroll A.) Deering" of Portland, Maine. She usually sailed the trade routes between her home port and Barbados, so it was not strange that in December 1920 she departed Portland for Rio de Janeiro with a general cargo.

The "Deering" arrived on schedule without incident, took on a new general cargo and started out on a return voyage. She was cleared for Norfolk, Virginia with a stop scheduled at Barbados. As had been the routine for many years, she arrived at the British West Indies port for further orders. When no change was received she set sail for Norfolk.

On January 29th, the schooner made contact with the Cape Lookout Lightship, North Carolina, asking that her "Managing Owners, G. G. Deering Company of Portland", be notified that she had lost both anchors. The request was made by a man other than the

"Deering's" Master, Captain Willis B. Wormwell. Otherwise, the schooner appeared to be in very good condition, sailing at a speed of about five nautical miles.

A short time later, a steamer, the name of which was not ascertained, was passing the Lightship when the Master of the Light signalled the vessel to stop in order to take a message for forwarding. In spite of numerous attempts to attract the steamer's attention, no response was given.

Two days later, January 31st, the "Carol Deering" was found washed ashore a few miles north of the Lightship at Diamond Shoals. Her crew of twelve officers and men were no where to be found.

Officials from the nearest life saving station boarded her and reported finding evidence that indicated abandonment took place in a hurry, yet for no conceivable reason. They noted that her motor-lifeboat and dory were gone and most of the provisions, clothing and supplies of the vessel had been removed. She was in good shape, her sails were fully set and the general cargo seemed to be untouched.

Coast Guard vessels began the search for survivors by slipping in and out of coves and inlets along the North Carolina coast in hope of picking up some clue - a bit of wreckage or a note which might have been left by a member of the "Deering's" crew. For seventy days the hunt was conducted and yet not a trace of the crew or wreckage of her small boats had been discovered.

CLUE FOUND - PIRACY SUSPECTED

On April 11, 1921, Christopher Columbus Ray reported that he found a bottle containing a message near his home at Buxton Beach, North Carolina, near Cape Hatteras. The unsigned note was believed written by the "Carol Deering's" mate, Engineer Henry Bates. The message read as follows: "Deering captured by oil-burning boat something like chaser, taking off everything, handcuffing crew. Crew hiding all over ship. No chance to make escape. Finder please notify headquarters of Deering."

FIVE GOVERNMENT DEPARTMENTS INVOLVED

On May 23, 1921, the Reverend Addison B. Lorimer, Pastor of the Central Square Baptist Church of Portland and Miss Lulu Wormwell, daughter of the "Deering's" Captain, sent a telegram to Senator Frederick Hale of Maine, asking for an appointment to see the Secretary of Commerce, Herbert Hoover. The telegram indicated that they had certain important facts relating to "piracy on the high seas."

The appointment was made, they went to Washington and were seen by Secretary Hoover, Senator Hale, Secretary Hughes and Commodore Reynolds of the Coast Guard Services. Reverend Lorimer and Miss Wormwell presented compiled evidence concerning the disappearance of the "Deering's" crew, including the message purporting to have been written by the ship's mate, as well as other information pertaining to several additional ships that vanished within the period of one year.

The evidence seemed so conclusive that an investigation was started by five departments of the Washington Government:

State Department — instructed its consular officers at ports throughout the world to be on the lookout for several missing vessels or members of the alleged kidnapped crew of the "Carol Deering".

Treasury Department - through its Coast Guard and Lifesaving service, launched a gigantic search of the Atlantic coast of the United States and adjacent waters.

Navy Department - dispatched vessels to assist other agencies involved in the search.

Department of Commerce - through its Bureau of Navigation, joined in to help the attempt to lift the veil of mystery.

Department of Justice - assigned some of its best agents to the case, for the Government was working on the theory of "foul play" and that all of the incidents were possibly interrelated.

Government officials stated difficulty in believing that acts of piracy could have been committed in or near the territorial waters of the United States. But the circumstantial evidence pointed to the suspicion that all the mysterious happenings were brought about by persons willing to take the chance of committing old time piratical crimes.

Perhaps the cause for the piracy was sincere sympathy for the Soviets or the merely greedy objective of disposing of pirated cargoes at extremely high prices to authorities of Soviet Russia. Possibly Soviet sympathizers had seized the vessels and sailed them directly to Russian ports.

On June 22nd, officials of the Department of Commerce were considering asking the military for planes to patrol the little frequented stretches of coast near Cape Hatteras for some trace of the merchant vessels that mysteriously vanished there.

Government spokesmen stated that if pirates had raided the ships and murdered or captured the crews they would have had to leave some trace along the shores, either in the way of boats, wreckage or dead bodies. It was pointed out that because the disappearances extended over a one year period the raiding vessel or vessels would have needed a nearby base of operations. At no time did the officials declare positively that all of the missing ships were the victims of pirates or possibly Bolshevist sympathizers, but neither did they deny it.

MISSING VESSELS

I have compiled information about some of the vessels that mysteriously disappeared off the coast of the United States from April 1920 to April 1921. Four of them vanished in February 1921 and three of them sailed from Norfolk, Virginia at about the same time.

* * * * * *

PIRACY

The fate of the new wooden steamship, "William O'Brien", a vessel of 3,143 tons, under charter of the France and Canada Steamship Company, had long been a topic of discussion in shipping circles. She left New York on April 14, 1920, bound for Rotterdam. The following day she put back to port. Her Captain said that he had experienced trouble with his crew, but would not elaborate.

On the tide of the next morning the steamer made a fresh start. A few days later on Sunday, April 18th, the steamer "Baltic" received a radio message from the "O'Brien" to the effect that she was 500 miles east of the Delaware River and needed assistance. Help was sent, but the freighter was never heard from again.

Three months later the mother of a member of the crew appeared at the office of the parent company with a postcard mailed in France and supposedly written in the hand of her son. It stated that he had been on a ship with Edsel Ford, son of Henry Ford. An investigation brought out the fact that the younger Ford was in Detroit at the time.

* * * * * *

Russian bark "Albyan" sailed from Norfolk on October 1, 1920. She was never heard from again and not the slightest trace of any wreckage was ever found.

* * * * * *

British schooner "General Morne" sailed from Lisbon for Newfoundland on October 19, 1920 and disappeared.

* * * * * *

Spanish steamer "Yute", of 2,974 tons, sailed from Baltimore on November 14, 1920. On November 17th she was heard calling for help and gave her position as about 240 miles off the New Jersey coast southeast of Cape May. Government vessels and other ships put out to her assistance, but were unable to find any trace.

* * * * * *

Norwegian bark "Flonine" left Hampton Roads on November 25, 1920 and disappeared.

* * * * * *

American steel steamer "Hewitt" of Portland, Maine, disappeared under equally mysterious circumstances. She sailed from Sabine, Texas on January 20, 1921, bound for Boston and Portland with a cargo of sulphur. She was sighted about 250 miles north of Jupiter Inlet, Florida, but that was the last to be seen of her. Government authorities were unable to find any trace. Not a boat or a spar had come ashore or had been picked up, and not a body of any member of her crew was found.

There was a remote possibility that the "Hewitt" might have been off Diamond Shoals about the same time the "Deering" went ashore. The Department of Commerce officials conjectured the "Hewitt" was still afloat and intact. Clarence A. Snider, Secretary of the Union Sulphur Company, owners of the steamer said, "I do not believe that the "Hewitt" is still afloat nor intact. We would have heard of her long before this. Anyway, we have collected the insurance on the craft." She was officially posted as missing on March 16, 1921.

* * * * * *

Italian steamer "Monte San Michele", of 4,061 tons, left Portland with a cargo of grain for Genoa on February 2, 1921 and disappeared.

* * * * * *

British tank steamer "Ottawa" departed Port Lobos bound for Manchester, England. She stopped at Norfolk, Virginia, and sailed from there on February 2, 1921. The steamer was in radio communication on February 6th with the steamer "Dorlington Court". Since then she has never been heard from.

* * * * * *

Brazilian steamer "Cabedello" sailed from Norfolk on February 3, 1921 and disappeared.

* * * * * *

British schooner "Esperenza de Larrinaga" also sailed from Norfolk on February 3, 1921 and likewise disappeared.

* * * * * *

British schooner "Canadian Maid" sailed from Monte Cristo for New York on April 4, 1921 and disappeared.

PIRACY THEORIES

Speculation as to what was going on at sea ran rampant. Everyone with the slightest bit of information had a theory.

* * * * * *

In May 1921, prior to contacting Secretary Hoover, Miss Wormwell told Harry C. Deering, of the firm that owned the derelict schooner, that she was going to ask for a Government investigation relative to her theory of "piracy on the high seas." Mr. Deering replied that if an investigation was conducted he would have little faith in the outcome.

* * * * * *

Captain William H. Merritt of South Portland, the "Deering's" original commander said he would help Miss Wormwell, but he also was not impressed with the chances of a piracy investigation ever producing any concrete results.

* * * * * *

Carroll A. Deering, for whom the schooner was named, remarked that twentieth century pirates had excellent opportunity to work by purchasing naval craft being offered for sale. He said that under favorable circumstances, and because of the general belief that piracy was non-existent, it could possibly be carried on undisturbed for a long time.

* * * * * *

On June 21st, members of the G. G. Deering Company stated they were not inclined to take seriously the theory that the "Carol Deering" was attacked by pirates, nor that Captain Wormwell and his crew were taken off and the vessel then allowed to sail along unmanaged.

* * * * * *

Captain O. O. W. Parker, Marine Superintendent of the Shipping Board, put his feeling this way, "Piracy without a doubt still exists, and it has since the days of the Phoenicians."

* * * * * *

Many ship owners said that it seemed unlikely that sea robbers could have preyed on thirteen ships without the fact becoming known. In support of their contention, they pointed out that the use of on board wireless radio apparatus was becoming almost universal. Also, the commerce lanes of the ocean were more crowded than ever before and there was an international patrol which kept a close watch on things.

* * * * * *

Many other shipping owners, especially those familiar

with sailing vessels and tramp steamers, gave credence to the opinion held by Washington officials that piracy was again being practiced, or that agents of Soviet Russia were seizing craft on the ocean.

* * * * * *

Commodore Reynolds of the Coast Guard Services said that it was not likely that the men of the "Carol Deering" were taken to any South American or any accessible European port. In his opinion the crew had not been landed anywhere. He suggested that there might have been a mutiny on an oil tanker, whose crew put the men of the "Deering" in irons and carried them away to parts unknown, or murdered them.

* * * * * *

At this point I must add my own views. The theory of regular pirates cannot pass for more than the remotest of possibilities.

As for Red sympathizers acting as pirates for Soviet Russia, this certainly has been disproved by history alone. Let's assume Russian port pirates did exist. They would have been operating against world shipping, and their stolen cargoes would have had to be landed and sold. Doubtless there were men who would deal in stolen goods and not care how they had been obtained. But in those days, as today, shipping regulations throughout the world were against such traffic, making it too difficult and dangerous to be practical. So let's go on the assumption that the pirates tried to carry their bounty back to Russia. I cannot believe that they were able to get through the Baltic or into the Black Sea undetected.

MUTINY THEORY

On June 21, 1921, Senator Hale of Maine, who first asked for a Government investigation of the disappearance of the "Hewitt" and of the "Carol Deering's" crew, advanced the theory that mutiny and not piracy was the explanation of the sea mysteries. He declared that he did not take any stock in reports that a Russian or other submarine raider was in operation. He called attention to the statement in the unsigned message in the bottle, that the "Deering's" crew had been taken off forcibly by another ship. He said, "I think it will be found to be a plain case of mutiny in at least one of the cases. Possibly the mutinous crew of one vessel boarded the other to get a navigator." It was a well known fact that the "Deering's" Captain was an excellent and thoroughly reliable navigator.

STORMS AND NATURAL DISASTER THEORIES

Many shipping men believed the disappearances of the vessels in question were caused by natural accidents rather than the activities of pirates or Bolshevist marauders. They insisted that the fate of some of the missing vessels were attributed to hitting mines, icebergs, derelicts and storms.

*　*　*　*　*　*

On June 23rd, weather bureau officials came forward with a theory that some of the ships that vanished had fallen victim to a series of unusually severe storms which were known to have swept certain areas of the Atlantic during the first weeks of February, 1921. The weather bureau theorized that during a forbidding storm the "Deering's" crew left their vessel in small boats and were lost. In contradiction weather bureau files also contained reports from a number of ships which passed through the February disturbances and reached port safely.

PIRATE TALE A FAKE

On August 25, 1921, Lawrence Richey, Special Assistant to the Secretary of Commerce stated that the investigation by the five Government departments was completed. Stories that the schooner "Carol Deering" had been captured by pirates of the Soviet Government of Russia were put to rest once and for all.

The report showed evidence that the mysterious note alleged to have been found in a bottle, telling the fantastic tale of capture by pirates, was a fake. Investigation proved that the bottle was of California manufacture and the paper was made in America. It was also determined that because the bottle was of one pint capacity and had an extremely narrow neck, that it would have been virtually impossible to get the paper out without first breaking the bottle.

Christopher Columbus Ray, who reported the

discovery of the bottle, was interviewed by investigators of the government. His handwriting on the note and on letters he had sent to the Customs officials at Norfolk, Virginia were inspected. Government agents were satisfied that Ray had written both. Finally, after long hours of questioning, Ray admitted that the note did not come from the "Carol Deering". He told a story about fishermen on the North Carolina coast having prepared it. Thus the bottle and note were finally accounted for.

SUMMARY

Messages found in bottles thrown overboard from ships sinking or otherwise in desperate trouble have figured prominently in many an ocean tale. They have, of course, also played a part in some real tragedies of the sea, but the stories have been more numerous than the realities. It is also a fact that landsmen accept such tales more readily than experienced seafarers.

The five Government departments handled the "note in the bottle" nicely. They sifted all available evidence in order to get to the bottom of the whole mystery, and yet in the end they had to admit failure.

What did happen to the "Carol Deering" and the other twelve vessels and their crews? Strange as it may seem, to this day nobody has ever been able to come up with an absolute answer. I believe the key to the secret lies within the "Limbo of the Lost".

BLACKBEARD THE PIRATE

While researching the story surrounding the "Carol Deering", I found myself wondering what kind of person a real pirate was. I've always imagined a pirate as a sort of swashbuckler, the Errol Flynn type who was always burying a treasure on some south sea island beach. To satisfy my curiosity I selected probably the most picturesque of all pirates to study - Edward Teach, the infamous "Blackbeard".

Supposedly Teach was born in or near Bristol, England, and during his short lifetime gained a reputation for being an accomplished sea captain. Although his career as an independent commander under the skull and crossbones lasted only about three years, from 1716 to 1718, he seemed to have performed sufficient curious and atrocious deeds to give him a place more prominent than that accorded to more gentlemanly rogues, who followed their chosen calling for half an ordinary lifetime. He was a most hardened villain, bold and daring to the last degree.

His name was due to his great remarkably black ugly beard which like a frightful demon covered his whole face. His gruesome whiskers were the pride of his life. We are told he trained and curled and nursed them until they were as luxuriant and almost as artificial in appearance as the great powdered wigs of the day. His appearance caused more terror on the high seas than any weapon.

Teach started his operations with St. Thomas as his base, but soon shifted to Nassau. From there he sailed for the coast of Virginia. On his way he captured three vessels, among them a large French ship which he took for his own. Naming her the "Queen Anne's Revenge", he armed the man-of-war with forty large cannons and set out to accomplish, off the North American mainland, just what he had done among the islands.

Early in 1717 he ran aground off the coast of North Carolina and surrendered to Governor Charles Eden, a British official of the Colonies. Some historians say a partnership was formed between Teach and the unsavory Governor in which he was to give the Governor part of the proceeds of the spoils from his raids. Blackbeard made his permanent headquarters at Edenton, North Carolina, where he operated with two large privateers and a small sloop which served as a tender.

During stormy nights Blackbeard's men would tie a lantern to a horse's head and send the steed trotting up and down the coast to lure craft ashore, in the belief that the bobbing light, from seaward, would appear as that of a vessel in deep water. Because of these reported tales this area of North Carolina has been officially named "Nag's Head".

Blackbeard not only had the chief rule, but the greatest control over his men of any pirate Captain ever known. He would perpetrate the most abominable wickedness imaginable just to prove he was a man of blood and iron. Aware that no pirate Captain was safe over his command unless he was known as the strongest hand on the vessel, he continually and deliberately practiced maltreatment of his men so that there might be no doubt as to who was master.

Many stories with many variations have been told of how he killed and wounded his own men simply to remind them that he was in authority. Teach use to invite a couple of his crew to drink with him in his cabin. While the bowl was passing, he would cock a pair of the twelve pistols he always carried, blow out the candle, and then fire under the table. A crew member who came out of this game with a shattered knee asked the meaning of it. "Damn you, snapped Blackbeard, if I didn't kill one of you now and again, you'd forget who I am."

Blackbeard's authority owed more to his daily villainies than to the rooted belief of his followers that he was in league with and protected by the devil himself. One day he perpetrated an insane incident by turning the hold of his ship into what he was pleased to call "a little hell." The various accounts agree that he took some of his favorite followers below deck, and there proceeded to burn sulphur and brimstone, all the while drinking goblets of rum and howling as he imagined the devil might shriek in a happy environment. He was just testing the stay powers of his men, and when he proved he could remain in the sulphur laden fumes longer than any of them he proudly declared this was proof of his identity with the devil. With his half crazed desire to be mistaken for the "evil one", Teach was a real living dime store novel character.

Blackbeard and his men lurked about the mouth of the James River and preyed on coastal shipping trade. After a successful raid he would run his small fleet back through the few and dangerous inlets, past the narrow sandbars that separate the Atlantic Ocean from the sounds that front on the North Carolina mainland.

In November 1718, Governor Alexander Spottiswood of Virginia organized an expedition against Blackbeard at the urgent requests of Virginia planters. Lieutenant Robert Maynard of the British Navy was chosen to lead a small convoy to trap and bring to justice one, Edward Teach.

After careful naval planning he engaged Blackbeard in combat. With his entire crew Teach boarded the British man-of-war with a pistol in one hand and a cutlass in the other, but not until he had received sixteen wounds by shot and steel did he finally die.

Lieutenant Maynard cut off the pirate's head and placed it on the bowspit of his vessel. With Teach's great black beard flowing in the sea breeze, the British vessel sailed into port to show everyone that the scourge of the merchants and planters was no more. A wealthy man obtained the skull and had it silvered for the purpose of making a drinking mug out of it.

Blackbeard left fourteen wives, countless children and buried treasure which to this day has not been found.

CHAPTER VII

POSSIBLE EXPLANATION
AND
LATEST LOSSES

DO SEA SERPENTS REALLY EXIST?

The stories about gigantic sea monsters may not be just simply tales told by superstitious mariners after all. Because of recent discoveries, many scientists have very good reasons for believing in the existence of giant sea serpents.

* * * * * *

Dr. Robert J. Menzies, University of Southern California marine biologist was credited with the discovery of the "Neopilina", a very small sea animal that was believed extinct for over 300 million years.

* * * * * *

Dr. Anton F. Bruun, lecturer on Oceanology at the University of Copenhagen, Denmark, reported that on a night in February, 1930, off the southwest coast of Africa, between the Cape of Good Hope and the small island of St. Helena he captured, in a net, a six-foot-long "Leptocephalus" (baby eel). He said it had a small pointed head, with long fangs in its jaws, and seemed to be a typical "larval eel" in all respects except for its gigantic size. If the same ratio of growth that was known of other members of the eel family were applied, the parents of the two-yard eel would be at least a length of thirty to fifty feet.

* * * * * *

Professor L. R. Richardson of Victoria University in New Zealand reported finding an immature larval eel three feet long. The baby eel had a reptilian head, large sharp teeth and well developed eyes. It was believed to be a different species than Dr. Bruun's discovery, however the projected size of its parents would also be very large, possibly about 30 feet.

* * * * * *

Captain Peter M'Quhae in command of the British frigate "Daedalus" was sailing in the Atlantic between the Cape of Good Hope and St. Helena on August 6, 1848. At 5:00 p.m. his crew called his attention to an enormous, sixty-foot-long sea serpent. He reported that the monster passed rapidly, but so close, as he put it, "that had it been a man of my acquaintance, I should have easily recognized his features with the naked eye." The creature's southwest course never deviated and it held a pace of approximately 12 to 15 miles per hour.

Captain M'Quhae said, "the diameter of the Serpent was about 15 or 16 inches behind the head, which was, without any doubt, that of a snake. Its color was dark brown, with yellowish white about the throat. It had no fins, but something like the mane of a horse, or rather, a bunch of seaweed, washed about its back."

* * * * * *

The Master of the American brig "Daphne" in South Atlantic waters on September 20, 1848 reported seeing "a most extraordinary animal about 100 feet long . . . . the appearance of a huge serpent or snake."

When the serpent was a distance of only 40 yards from the "Daphne" they fired a deck gun loaded with spikes at it. The monster reared its head in the air and plunged violently, foaming and lashing the water. As the ship approached, the brute, although wounded, raced off at fifteen or sixteen knots.

* * * * * *

Two British Zoologists, Michael J. Nicoll and E. G. B. Meade-Waldo were aboard the yacht "Valhalla", off Parahiba, Brazil, on December 7, 1905. At about 10:00 a.m. the two zoologists saw a large fin or frill, somewhat crinkled at the edge, sticking out of the water.

The monster had a great turtle-like head, the neck was about as thick as a man's body and it rose about seven or eight feet out of the water. The color of the head and neck, which moved from side to side in a strange manner, was dark seaweed brown above and whitish below. The yacht quickly sailed away from the strange creature which was traveling very slowly.

* * * * * *

LATEST LOSSES

The Captain of the Grace Liner, "Santa Clara" reported that he and his crew sighted a snakelike sea serpent at 11:55 a.m. on December 30, 1947, while they were steaming southwest through the calm waters about 120 miles east of Cape Lookout, North Carolina.

The dark brown, slick and smooth monster was first spotted thirty feet off the starboard bow. As it approached abeam of the bridge, the witnesses noticed blood staining an area thirty to forty square feet around the creature. The visible part of its body was about 35 feet long. Presumably the stem of their ship had cut the snakelike monster in two. No fins, hair, or protuberances on the head, neck or visible parts of the body could be seen.

From the time the serpent was first sighted until it vanished in the distance, it thrashed about as though in agony.

SCOTLAND'S NOTORIOUS LOCH NESS MONSTER

Loch Ness, the largest mass of fresh water in the United Kingdom, is said to be inhabited by an aquatic monster, accounts of which have been publicized since the early 1930's.

The quiet 700 square miles of lake stretches southwest and northeast 24 miles, has a uniform width of about a mile and depths of 754 feet. Nestled in Scotland's bonnie highlands, six miles from Inverness, the famous ice-free lake is fed by several large rivers known for salmon fishing.

The unidentified swimming object, affectionately named "Nessie" by its seekers, is not known to be a "he" or a "she". Many people scoff at its existence while others are firm believers. Speculation on what it might actually be range from a submarine to some sort of curiosity left over from prehistoric days.

Many scientists believe there is little doubt that something is in the Loch. In fact, they think there may be a whole clan of somethings breeding in the murky water of the lake.

A movie film taken in 1959 has been analyzed by the British Joint Air Reconnaissance Intelligence Center (JARIC). The JARIC experts are recognized as among the world's best photographic interpreters. They took measurements on every frame of the film, taking into consideration light conditions, reflections, the angle of the object and the position of the camera.

Their conclusions? The object was not a surface vessel, nor was it a submarine; "leaving the conclusion that it probably is an animate object." It was moving along at about ten miles an hour. By a series of measurements and reasonings, the experts deduced that the object, though most of it was beneath the surface, was approximately 92 feet long, not less than six feet wide, and not more than five feet high.

That description would seem to fit "sea serpent" rather well. British Air Defense Minister, Lord Shackleton, commented on the JARIC finding: "I have always disbelieved in the Loch Ness Monster, but now I am even more mystified. I find it difficult to discount the finding of this report."

* * * * * *

Up to five hundred members of the "Phenomena Investigation Bureau, Limited", take turns camping out on the shores of the Loch every year, from the middle of March to the middle of October.

Armed with field-glasses, long pads and 35-millimeter movie cameras with telephoto lenses, they keep a record of anything that moves on the lake. According to observers' reports, "Nessie" has been ·sighted many times. But a clear, well-focused, unmistakable picture has yet to be taken at least as of this writing.

* * * * * *

The sightings haven't all been in recent years, either. Local legends go back centuries, including one involving Saint Columba, the Abbot of Iona. He made the first recorded sighting in 565 A.D. According to the Chronicles, "the Holy man gave a great shout and commanded the beast to go back into the depths from which he came." The monster obligingly did so and ever since, one of its often reported characteristics has been a fear of noise.

* * * * * *

A retired British Navy officer, Lieutenant Commander Francis Flint of Burgess Hill, Sussex, said he knows it's actually there because he hit it in 1943 and damaged his motor launch. He said he didn't actually see the monster, but he didn't see anything else that could have caused the jolting impact or damage to his launch either.

* * * * * *

Attempts to locate "Nessie" by sonar have failed in the past because of the echoes from the steep underwater walls of the Loch. In the summer of 1968 a new kind of sonar was tried, developed by engineers at England's University of Birmingham. It uses a computer to screen out the confusing echoes, and during testing it found something large and moving in the depths of Loch Ness.

* * * * * *

A favorite theory is that "Nessie" is a descendant of some big-bodied, long-necked reptile (lizards or eels), called "Plesiosaurs", which roamed the steamy world of more than 100 million years ago. How the "Plesiosaur" survived the succession of ice ages since isn't explained.

A less romantic theory is that the Loch Ness monster is a full grown specimen of one of those giant eel larvae which oceanographers occasionally fish up from the ocean depths.

* * * * * *

The British government still maintains an official disbelief in "Nessie", but for some unknown reason a law was placed on the books in 1934 officially protecting the non-existent monster of Loch Ness from harm by hunters.

Whatever "Nessie" might be, the Scots have forbidden anyone from harming her. They say they would most vigorously oppose any attempt by anyone to touch one hair of its hide, that is supposing it has hair or for that matter, a hide.

M/V SOUTHERN CITIES LOST IN GULF
SATURDAY, OCTOBER 29, 1966

At approximately 11:45 on the night of October 29, 1966, the 85 gross tons, 67 foot tug boat "M/V Southern Cities" departed Freeport, Texas. She was bound for Tuxpan, Mexico, with six persons on board and a 210 foot loaded barge in tow astern on a hawser. This was her fifth voyage since July 25th when a verbal contract with Bludworth Marine Equipment Company, Houston, Texas and the "Southern Cities' " owner, F. W. Towing Company, Inc., Bella Chasse, Louisiana was initiated. The agreement called for the towing of the 1,013 gross ton, sea-going bulk cargo barge number B-1800 between Freeport and Tuxpan.

Three days after setting out on her last voyage the "Southern Cities' " owner received a report from the tug's Master stating that she was 95 miles south of Port Isabel, Texas - 43 miles offshore and 230 miles to go. She was making six knots, the weather was fine, no problems were being experienced and it was estimated she would arrive at Tuxpan on the morning of Thursday, November 3rd. It was further acknowledged that another report would be made the next morning.

It was to be relayed through the "M/V Texan", another tug located approximately 18 miles southeast of Tuxpan attending a Mexican Government drilling barge.

On the morning of November 2nd, the "Southern Cities" owner was notified that no report had been received. The following morning the Company was again advised that no report had been received from their vessel. Shortly thereafter, at 8:34, the U. S. Coast Guard Rescue Coordination Center in New Orleans, Louisiana was contacted by the "Southern Cities" owner and a formal request for aircraft assistance in locating and establishing communications with the missing tug was initiated.

SEARCH STARTED

An air search of 8,400 square miles was made along the estimated tow route north of Tuxpan. When nothing was located an intensive hunt began, covering a line from a position fifteen miles off Vera Cruz, Mexico, to Tuxpan. In addition an area from Tuxpan to Latitude 24° North, about fifteen to forty miles off the coast, was scanned by air and surface craft.

At 8:33 on the morning of November 5th, barge B-1800 was located by search craft drifting 105 miles north of Tuxpan. The barge was undamaged, there was no mark of recently caused indentations, and her cargo of bulk soda ash, caustic and amines contained in drums of various sizes, was intact. The 600 foot long, eight inch polypropylene tow line was still made fast to the barge, and the chafing chain and hawser, which were normally secured to the towing bitt of the "Southern Cities", were also intact.

At 2:05 in the afternoon of the same day that the barge was located, one adult cork life preserver was recovered 120 miles from Tampico, Mexico. In a near vicinity, two broken sections of a name board were recovered, and when fitted together bore the name "UTHERN CITIES". Also recovered was a 24 foot length of unraveled tow line. Several days later a ring lifebuoy was found approximately fifteen miles south of the Port Isabel, Texas jetties.

CONCLUSIONS

As in the disappearance of the "Marine Sulphur Queen" the few bits of debris only tended to confuse rather than assist the investigators. Negligence due to lack of safety precautions must be eliminated. She was given a thorough drydock check and overhaul at Houston a month and a half before her disappearance. The missing tug was equipped with a twenty-man balsa lifefloat, five - 30 inch ring life buoys, twelve life preservers and nine fire extinguishers. The "Southern Cities" was similar to the various designs of the ST (small tug) type harbor tugs built for the Army Transportation Corps during World War II. At the time of her disappearance her market value was estimated at $30,000, with a replacement cost of approximately $125,000.

The search was officially terminated as of dusk November 8th. The number of aircraft flights or sorties during the hunt was listed as forty-three, totaling 253.3 hours and covering 84,600 square miles. The last known reported position of the "Southern Cities" was used as the starting point in the search.

BOARD OF INVESTIGATION REPORT

On November 28, 1966 the Department of Transportation, United States Coast Guard, Marine Board of Investigation released a report which I quote in part:

"In the absence of survivors or physical remains of the ship, the exact cause of the loss of the "M/V Southern Cities" cannot be determined . . . Although there is no evidence indicating a failure of the vessel's radio equipment, the failure of the vessel to transmit a distress message appears to justify the conclusion that the loss of the vessel may have occurred so rapidly as to preclude the transmission of such a message . . . The six men (See Appendix K for names) are presumed dead as a result of the casualty. There has been no trace of them since the sinking. There is no probability that the vessel or any of the six persons on board will be recovered . . . "

"It is further concluded that there is no evidence of negligence, misconduct or foul play on the part of any of the crew members. There is no evidence of violation of laws or regulations enforced by the U. S. Coast Guard. It is finally concluded that there is no evidence that any personnel of the Coast Guard or any other government agency or any other person contributed to the casualty. It is recommended that the case be closed and no further action be taken."

Other than the few items found, no other debris or gear belonging to the "M/V Southern Cities" or her crew was ever located. It was as though she just foundered into the "Limbo of the Lost".

DEPARTMENT OF TRANSPORTATION
UNITED STATES COAST GUARD

Address reply to:

5943
M/V SOUTHERN CITIES
14, 28 November 1966

From: Marine Board of Investigation
To: Commandant (MVI)

Subj: M/V SOUTHERN CITIES, O.N. 241635; Disappearance in the Gulf of Mexico
on or about 1 November 1966, with loss of life

Findings of Fact:

1. At approximately 2345, +6 zone time, on 29 October 1966, the M/V SOUTHERN
CITIES, O.N. 241635, departed Freeport, Texas, bound for Tuxpan, Mexico, with
six (6) persons on board and with loaded barge B-1800, O.N. 293266, in tow
astern on a hawser. At approximately 0630 on 1 November 1966, the vessel reported her position as Latitude 24°-30'' North and Longitude 96°-40' West.
No further communication was received from the M/V SOUTHERN CITIES. At 0833,
on 5 November 1966, barge B-1800 was located drifting in position Latitude
22°-45' North and Longitude 97°-15' West. The M/V SOUTHERN CITIES was never
found, now were any of the six (6) persons that were on board.

2. The M/V SOUTHERN CITIES, O.N. 241635, was a welded steel single screw
diesel propelled towing vessel built in 1942 at Walker Shipyard, Pascagoula,
Mississippi, for the Southern Tug & Barge Company of New Orleans, Louisiana.
She was similar to the various designs of the ST type harbor tugs built for
the Army Transportation Corps during World War II. The M/V SOUTHERN CITIES,
of New Orleans, Louisiana, was powered by a 400 brake horsepower, 6 cylinder,
4 cycle air started, direct reversible Atlas Imperial diesel engine, engine-
room controlled. Her registered dimensions were 67 feet in length, 19.1 feet
in breadth and 7.7 feet in depth. She was of 85 gross tons and 57 net tons.
The vessel was owned and operated by F. W. Towing Company, Inc., of Box 232 E,
Belle Chasse, Louisiana. Frank Wyman, of the above address, was President.
The Master was Grady A. Reynolds, of 701 Forstall Street, New Orleans, Louisiana,
License 36372, operator of mechanically propelled vessels of 100 gross tons or
less on waters other than ocean or coastwise. The vessel was purchased from
Arkansas Navigation Company, Inc., of Box 207, Osceola, Arkansas, in February
1966. The SOUTHERN CITIES was not subject to inspection by the U. S. Coast
Guard, being under 300 gross tons, and had never been in class with a Classi-
fication Society. Also, the persons on board were not required to be licensed
or certificated. No stability data of the SOUTHERN CITIES could be obtained.

SCORPION MYSTERY STILL UNSOLVED

The nuclear-powered submarine, "U. S. S. Scorpion", valued at 40 million dollars, disappeared with its entire crew of ninety-nine officers and enlisted men while enroute home to the United States after a Mediterranean training operation in May, 1968.

An extensive search was conducted and on October 29th, some ten-thousand feet deep and 460 miles southwest of the Azores, her wreckage was located.

A court of inquiry report released in January, 1969 summarized that, despite twelve-thousand photographs of Atlantic floor debris, the U. S. Navy is still unable to say what happened to the sub.

After hearing ninety witnesses and piling up 1,334 pages of testimony during eleven weeks, the seven man court of inquiry said, "The certain cause of the loss of "Scorpion" cannot be ascertained from any evidence now available."

The court recommended a further effort be made to take closer photographs of the wreckage. In reply the Navy said they are pinning hope of solving the mystery on a deep-diving bathyscope, "Trieste II". On-the-spot observations have begun and additional close-up photographs of the "Scorpion's" hull will be taken.

The "Scorpion" is the worst submarine disaster since the "Thresher" was crushed after a piping failure off New England in 1963.

Until a confirmed explanation is given, I must consider this another mystery for the "Limbo of the Lost".

EPILOGUE

Incidents in the "Limbo of the Lost" occur only occasionally . . . without warning . . . without pattern . . . without explanation, but frequently enough to be alarming.

To this day the secret of the "Limbo of the Lost" is well kept!

APPENDICES

APPENDIX A

FIVE TBM-3 AVENGER TORPEDO BOMBERS... NAVY PATROL PLANES. MARTIN MARINER (PBM) FLYING BOAT... RESCUE PLANE...

DEC. 5, 1945 ... LOST - 27

At a press conference called on the morning of the 4th Anniversary of the bombing of Pearl Harbor the names of the missing fliers were released.

A typical example of the calibre and experience of the downed fliers was Marine Sergeant Robert Francis Gallivan, 21, of Northampton, Massachusetts. Gallivan was in the Marines for four years. He took his basic training at Paris Island, South Carolina early in 1942 and then transferred to the Marine Air Force. He was sent to the South Pacific where he served eighteen

147

months winning a Commendation Ribbon in addition to the American and Pacific Theater Ribbons. Gallivan returned to the United States in November 1945 and after a thirty day leave at home, reported to Cherry Point, North Carolina, then to Fort Lauderdale Naval Air Station, Florida.

Recently I talked to Mrs. Gallivan about the disappearance of her son. She told me that on December 6, 1945, she didn't go to work because it was the day Robert was to be home from the service for good.

Instead of her son, a telegram arrived from the War Department stating that he was missing at sea. Mrs. Gallivan sadly commented, when it was all over, that Navy officials only remarked that the disappearance of Robert Francis Gallivan was just one of those strange unsolved mysteries of the sea.

Other personnel among the fourteen officers and enlisted men on the patrol bombers were these:

Arm. 3/c Walter Reed Parpart, Jr., - Brooklyn, N.Y.
Arm. 3/c George F. Beulin - Brooklyn, N.Y.
Seaman 3/c Bert Edward Valuk, Jr., - Bloomfield, N.J.
Pfc. Robert Peter Gruebbl, USMC - Maspeth, N.Y.
Capt. Edward Joseph Powers, Jr., USMC - Vernon, N.Y.
S/Sgt. George Richard Paonessa, USMC - Mamaroneck, New York

Among the men on the missing Navy (PBM) search plane was:

Seaman 1/c P. S. Neeman - North Hill, Pa.

APPENDIX   B

SUPER CONSTELLATION . . . NAVY PASSENGER PLANE . . .

OCT. 30, 1954 . . . LOST - 42

List of Those on Plane

Aboard the ill fated Navy Super-Constellation were thirty-two naval personnel and two members of the Air Force. Half of the twenty-one air crewmen were slated to leave the flight at the Azores to pick up another plane. Seven of the eight civilians aboard were wives or children of service men.

Crew Members:
Lieut. Comdr. John S. Cole - Maryland
Hospitalman, third class John T. Davis - W. Va.
Aviation metalsmith, second class Gerald F. DeBoid - Maryland
Lieut. Herbert W. Eden - Maryland
Airman Frank J. Graziano - Pa.
Chief machinist's mate Eugene Huntley - Maryland
Lieut. Russell L. Klemetti - Maryland
Lieut. John G. Leonard - Maryland
Chief machinist's mate Frank T. Meidl - Maryland
Aviation radioman, second class Raymond R. Meyers - Illinois
Hospitalman, third class Noel R. Moore - Pa.
Lieut. Peter J. Mostika - Maryland
James R. Pflager - Maryland

Seaman Florence B. Reitkrentz - Wisc.
Johnny M. Roberts - Kansas
Lieut. Davis Roberts - Tenn.
Lieut. Rodney S. Sprigg, Jr. - Maryland
Seaman Louis H. Staley, Jr. - Maryland
Chief machinist's mate Robert Stephenson - N.J.
Machinist's mate Robert T. Thomas - Maryland
Seaman Marian L. Wolff - Calif.

Passengers:
Lieut. Gilbert Jacobson of Brooklyn, en route on Navy assignment to Port Lyautey with his wife and twin 2-year-old children.
Major Edward H. Adrian - Pa.
Chief dental technician Francis Earl Baker - Va.
Ensign Cornelius P. Collins - N.Y.
Radioman, first class John Edward Gregg - Kan.
David R. Harr - Port Lyautey, North Africa
Geraldine L. Harr - Port Lyautey, North Africa
Kathy A. Harr - Port Lyautey, North Africa
Timothy J. Harr - Port Lyautey, North Africa
Seaman Leonard Ray Hawvaker - Iowa
Major Joseph U. Herold - APO 117
Dental technician Valentine Muscarelli - Va.
George W. Pongonis, Jr. - N.J.
Chief machinist's mate Robert L. Ridle - Calif.
Ronald Larue Warren - Pa.
Billy Joe Wayne - W. Va.
Apprentice seaman George Owen Willingham - N.C.
Apprentice seaman James White - Pa.

MARTIN "MARLIN" . . . NAVY FLYING BOAT . . .

NOV. 9, 1956 . . . LOST - 10

The Navy in Washington announced the following men were aboard the plane, and as of Saturday, November 10th, were officially listed as missing:

Petty Officer 3/C Wendell F. Beverly - Williamston, Mass.
Petty Officer 3/C Billy G. Comer - Blossburg, Ala.
Petty Officer 3/C Jesse W. Grable - Centralia, Ill.
Petty Officer 3/C Richard W. Montgomery - Cynwyd, Pa.
Lieut. (j.g.) Charles W. Patterson - Bermuda
Petty Officer 2/C Lyle F. Quimby - Minneapolis, Minn.
Lieut. (j.g.) Cyrus E. Reid, Jr. - Dallas, Texas
Petty Officer 1/C Robert W. Taylor - West Liberty, Ohio
Comdr. John M. Sweeney - Warwick, Bermuda
Airman Bobbie L. Sanders - Houston, Texas

STAR TIGER . . . BRITISH PASSENGER PLANE . . .

JAN. 30, 1948 . . . LOST - 31

Names of Missing Passengers and Crew

Eighteen British:

Air Marshal Sir Arthur Coningham, Royal Air Force, who Commanded the Second Tactical Air Force of the Allies at the invasion of Normandy, was considered one of the world's foremost authorities on the use of tactical air power in cooperation with ground armies. Sir Arthur was on his way to Nassau and planned to spend a few days in Bermuda with Sir Richard Fairey, head of a British aircraft manufacturing company that bears his name.

Assistant Secretary of the British Treasury, H. Ernest Brooks. Mr. Brooks was bound for Bermuda on business.

Major and Mrs. A. T. Barwell - Argyll, Scotland

Thomas Walton Davies - Kelvedon, Essex, England

Eric Fisher - Totteridge - North London

Cyril Morton Hawley - Windsor, Bershire

Mr. and Mrs. Anthony John Mulligan and Thomas R. J. Mulligan - London

Mrs. Sylvia Nebel, Miss Edith Nebel and Manfred and Vilem Nebel - Langley, England

George Keith Riddock - London

Robert Charles Staley - Wallsend, Northumberland
Mrs. Georgina Strong - Dunfermline, Scotland
John Matthews Sutherland - Leigh-on-Sea, England

Two Czechoslovakians:
Elias Klein and his wife who gave an address in Havana,
    Cuba

One Swiss:
Harold Gordon Cabrett - Zurich, Switzerland

Two Mexicans:
One name unknown.
Mr. Ignacio Echegaray Jauregul mailed a letter to his
wife from Santa Maria airport. He told of having to wait
there 19 hours and added: "The weather is still bad. We
don't know whether we will leave within an hour, or
tomorrow or the next day, via New York. When we
came here we were being blown by a 100-kilo-
meter-an-hour wind and we were about to be blown to
Canada or down into the ocean."

DC-3 . . . CHARTER PASSENGER PLANE . . .

DEC. 28, 1948 . . . LOST - 30

Published List of Missing

The following is the official passenger list for the missing DC-3 charter plane. Destination of the passengers are listed as follows:

New York:
Hilda Rivera, 23, 55 West 48th St.
Ramon Alvarez, 21, 55 West 48th St.
Emilia Perez, 22, 112 East 96th St.
Edmundo Carriga, 21, 319 West 48th St.
Jacinto Mercado, 22, 319 West 48th St.
Juan Ortiz, 24, 319 West 48th St.
Francisco Sanchez, 29, 319 West 48th St.
Jose Sanabria, 20, 1744 Lexington Ave.
Maria Ayala, 27, 1744 Lexington Ave.
Irene Rivera, 27, 1744 Lexington Ave.
Juan Rivera Ortega, 28, 244 East 117th St.
Francisco Delgado, 34, 244 East 117th St.
Esther Santiago, 26, 108 East 111th St.
Felix Rodrigues, 28, 319 West 48th St.
Leoncio Perez, 55 West 48th St.

Miami:
Pedro Carrasquilla, 32   Antonio Munoz, 24

Cenare Figueroa, 20   Vidal Rodriguez, 30
Juan M. Perez, 23   Ramon Rodriguez, 30
Carmen Vazquez, 22   Carmela Valesquez, 28

Lorain, Ohio:
Florencio Rivera, 38   Juan Rodriguez, 30

Two babies were also aboard.

APPENDIX F

STAR ARIEL . . . BRITISH PASSENGER PLANE . . .

JAN. 17, 1949 . . . LOST - 19

Names of Missing

R. Demire Quesada - Peruvian
Miss J. Muntalvo - Spanish
E. Murchard - British
T. Duboisson - British
F. Burthroyd - British
Mrs. R. Bentham Green - British
Miss J. Hodge - British
E. Stevens - British
H. S. Stewart - British
Group Captain H. Saker - British
Mrs. Marshall Meade and 2 year old son - Jamaica

The names of six crew members were given as:

J. McPhee, Captain - pilot

F. Dauncey - first officer

V. Shapley - second officer

G. Rettie - radio officer

K. Coleman - steward

J. Moxon - stewardess

APPENDIX G

KC-135A . . . MILITARY JET TANKERS (2) . . .

AUG. 28, 1963 . . . KILLED - 11

Names of Missing Crew Members

Plane One:

Capt. Allen C. Ferguson, 29, Elgin, Ill. (pilot)

Capt. Donald G. Edson, 30, No address available

Capt. Julius O. Womack, 30, Pioneer, La.

Capt. Gerald Gardner, 28, Lincoln, Neb.

1st Lt. Melvin C. Pump, 29, No address available

T/Sgt. Raymond L. Fish, 30, LaCrosse, Wisc.

Plane Two:

Capt. Richard A. Larson, 34, Minneapolis, Minn.(pilot)

Capt. Keith R. Goffin, 29, Bellevue, Ill.

1st Lt. William E. Smith, 26, Memphis, Tenn.

M/Sgt. Carl H. Burris, 39, Danube, Calif.

S/Sgt. Lyle E. Overlees, 25, Fulda, Minn.

Names of Missing

Officials at Langley Air Force Base released the names of these missing crewmen:

Maj. Robert J. Tawney - Middletown, Ohio (pilot)
Capt. Bernard A. Hanley - Jersey City, N.J. (navigator)
M/Sgt. Arnold W. Womak - Rassville, Ga. (flight eng.)
T/Sgt. Harry Stetser - Donora, Pa. (crew chief)
S/Sgt. Billie D. Moore - Tulsa, Okla. (refueling tech.)
A/3C William J. Anderson - San Bernardino, Calif.
    (assistant crew chief)
A/2C Carlton A. Link - Tampa, Fla. (refueling spec.)
A/2C Paul M. Clawson - Pacific, Calif. (refueling spec.)
1st Lt. Zoltan R. F. Szaloki - Whitinsville, Mass.
    (co-pilot)

APPENDIX I

C-54 ... ARMY CARGO TRANSPORT PLANE ...

JULY 3, 1947 ... LOST - 6

In an official statement the Commanding Officer of Kindley Field, Bermuda released the names of the following men, all members of his command:

Maj. Ralph B. Ward, Pilot - also operations director of Kindley Field - Concord, N.H.

Maj. Clyde R. Inman, Co-pilot - Boise, Idaho

Maj. John R. Sands, Jr. - Navigator - Jacksonville, Fla.

S/Sgt. Andrew S. Bagacus - Aerial Engineer - Townsend, Wisc.

Sgt. Fred E. Fricks - Assistant Aerial Engineer - Chattanooga, Tenn.

S/Sgt. Ernest D. Fey - Radio Operator - New Orleans, La.

Wives of all men lived in Bermuda as well as the son of Major Inman and the son and daughter of Sgt. Fricks.

APPENDIX J

SS MARINE SULPHUR QUEEN ... T2-SE-A1 TYPE TANK SHIP ...

FEB. 4, 1963 ... LOST - 39

The following is a complete crew list of the vessel:

James V. Fanning, Master - Beaumont, Tex.
George E. Watson, Chief Mate - Galveston, Tex.
Henry P. Hall, 2nd Mate - Beaumont, Tex.
Frank J. Cunningham, 3rd Mate - Beaumont, Tex.
George E. Sloat, Radio Officer - Baltimore, Md.
Leon B. Clauser, Chief Engineer - Beaumont, Tex.

John L. Denton, 1st Asst. Engineer - Friendswood, Tex.
A. R. Van Sickle, 2nd Asst. Engineer - Baltimore, Md.
E. W. Schneeberger, 3rd Asst. Engineer - Beaumont, Tex.
Adam Martin, Jr., 3rd Asst. Engineer - Austin, Tex.
Evans Phillips, Bosun - Tampa, Fla.
Ceburn R. Cole, DM/AB - Lake Charles, La.
Jack R. Schindler, AB - Seattle, Wash.
Fred A. Bodden, AB - Philadelphia, Pa.
Everett E. Arnold, AB - Memphis, Tenn.
Willie T. Manuel, AB - Ville Platte, La.
James Mck. Bodden, AB - Tampa, Fla.
Nelaton E. Devine, AB - Port Arthur, Tex.
John M. Nieznajski, OS - Gary, Ind.
Clarence Mcguire, OS - Bronsen, Tex.
James Phillips, OS - Port Arthur, Tex.
Jesse I. Vicera, Pumpman - Linden, N.J.
Alejandro Valdez, Oiler - Port Arthur, Tex.
John C. Ardoin, Oiler - Beaumont, Tex.
John Elmer Grice, Oiler - Daytona Beach, Fla.
Henry Clark, FWT - Jersey City, N.J.
Alphan Tate, FWT - Philadelphia, Pa.
Leroy Courville, FWT - Groves, Tex.
John Husch, Jr., Wiper - Akron, Ohio
Aaron Heard, Wiper - Norfolk, Va.
Juan Santos, Wiper - Newark, N.J.
Charles L. Dorsey, Chief Steward - Bronx, N.Y.
Vincent Thompson, Chief Cook - Baltimore, Md.
Cornelius Smith, 2nd Cook & Baker - Port Arthur, Tex.
Hugh D. Hunter, Galleyman - Chapel Hill, N.C.
Walter Pleasant, Messman - Port Arthur, Tex.

Wesley Fontenot, Messman - Mamou, La.
Robert E. Harold, Utilityman - Norfolk, Va.
Leroy B. Green, Utilityman - Rahway, N.J.

APPENDIX   K

M/V SOUTHERN CITIES ... TUG BOAT ...

NOV. 1, 1966 ... LOST - 6

A list of the six missing crew members are as follows:

Grady A. Reynolds, 27, Master - New Orleans, La.
Victor L. Benton, 41, Mate - Omega, Ga.
Clyde Wesley Sparkman, 45, Engineer - Houston, Tex.
George R. Johnson, 38, Deckhand - Jacksonville, Fla.
Buddy Lee, 45, Deckhand - Perry, Fla.
Thomas E. Rollins, 40, Deckhand - Perry, Fla.

All of the above persons were employed by F. W. Towing Company, Inc., owners of the "M/V Southern Cities".